A Village Airfield at War

Ken Wells

To. Gordon.

Best Wishes

Ken Wells

Steeple Morden. June. 93'

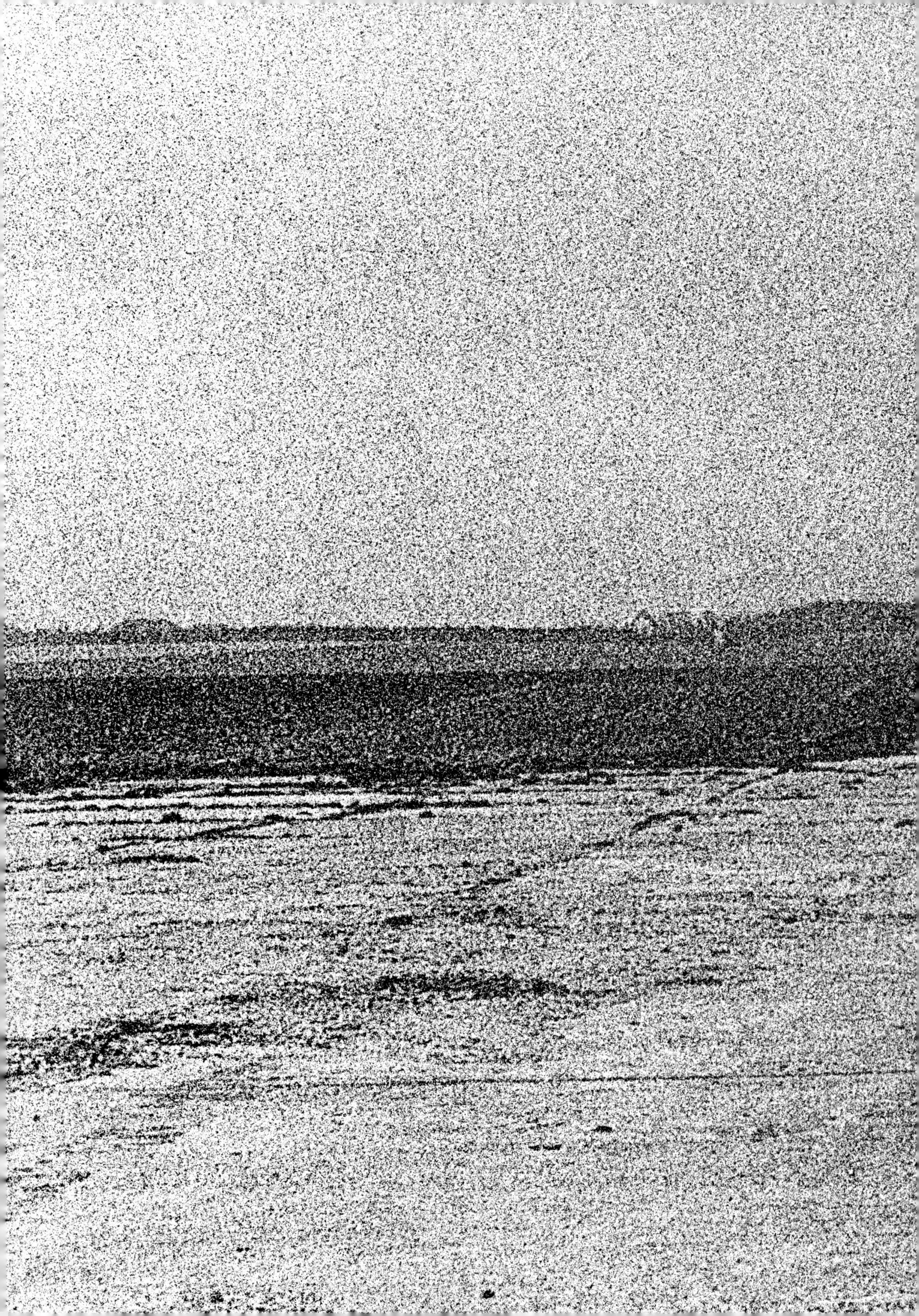

A
Village Airfield
at War

Ken Wells

Egon Publishers

First published May 1993
Egon Publishers Ltd, Royston Road, Baldock, Herts SG7 6NW

Copyright © Egon Publishers Ltd
ISBN 0 905858 87 5

Designed and typeset by BookEns Limited
for Egon Publishers Ltd

Printed in England by
Streetsprinters, Royston Road, Baldock, Herts SG7 6NW

Previous page:
Looking up at what is still left of
the main No I NE/SW runway at
Steeple Morden. In the background is the gap in the woods
that was cut to make take-offs
and landings easier.
(*Author*)

Contents

A fold-out plan of the Airfield dated May 1945 can be found at the end of the book.

Acknowledgements

Sincere thanks are due to the following individuals who contributed information and photographs: Mr Harry Hart; Mr J. Sharp, ex-11 OTU; Mr Jim Powling, ex-11 OTU; Mr John Deller; Mr Vince Hemmings (Curator, Tower Museum, Bassingbourn); Mr R. A. Beeton; Brian Sawford; Mr Alan Thorpe (John Laing Plc); Mr Ken Day, ex-17 OTU; Mr R. Rowland, ex-11 OTU; Flt Lt A. W. Simmonds, ex-11 OTU; Mr F. Mason, ex-11 OTU; Flt Lt Cotteral, ex-11 OTU; Sqn Ldr Stan Conway, ex-11 OTU; Flt Lt Tim Holden; Mrs M. Dickinson; Mr Don Hitch; Mr Lew Hitch; Mr Fred Hitch; Frank and Muriel Huffer; Mr John Savage; Mr Peter Jarman and Mr Ken Jarman; Mr Charlie Crow; Mr David Crow; Mr Bob Kuhnert, ex-355th FG; Mrs Doris Foster; Mr Stan Izzard; Mr and Mrs Charlie Potten; John and Avis Brocket; Mr V. Keeble, ex-11 OTU; Mr W. S. Andrews, ex-11 OTU; Mrs Patsy Briers; Mr A. W. Mills, ex-11 OTU; Mr J. W. Redfern, ex-11 OTU; Mr N. F. Kirby, DFC & Bar, ex-11 OTU; Mr W. Artist, ex-11 OTU; Mrs M. A. Riggs (WRAF); Mr R. G. Smith, ex-11 OTU; Mr G. F. Stanford, ex-11 OTU; Mr and Mrs Quirk, ex-11 OTU; Mr G. Taylor, ex-11 OTU; Mrs Sheila Allen, Mrs Audrey Newman, Mr Archie Harper, ex-11 OTU; Mr A. W. Hooper, ex-11 OTU; Mr Jock Whitehouse; Mr Harold Coates, ex-11 OTU; Mr George Paice, ex-11 OTU; Mr F. E. Ford, ex-11 OTU; Wg Cdr S. R. Hodge, ex-11 OTU; Mr Frank Page, ex-11 OTU; Mr M. J. Bowyer; Mr R. Houghton, ex-11 OTU; Mr Eric Gurney; Mr Fred Amore, ex-17 OTU; Mr Geoff Whittell, ex-11 OTU; Mr John Rowland, ex-11 OTU; Mr R. Holden ex-11 OTU; Mr John F. Hamlin; Mr J. R. White; Mr Roger Saunders; Mr Bob Richardson; Mr Simon Parry; Mr Alan Barker; Mr and Mrs Wilmott; Mr and Mrs Hunter; Mr Aubrey Wright; P/O M. Dickenson, ex-11 OTU; Mr H. Dawson; Sqn Ldr Ray Leach,

MBE; Sqn Ldr P.J.S. Boggis, DFC; Mr Gerry Tyack (Wellington Aviation Art), ex-11 OTU; Sqn Ldr John W. Gee, DFC; Sqn Ldr W.J.E. Craigen, ex-11 OTU; Mr J. Hampton; Sqn. Ldr Peter Singleton (MoD), Mr Lionel Hughes Ex. 11 OTU., Mr Reg Rogerson Jnr., Mr Michael Revels, Mr David Ellison, Mr Phil Crump, Mr Jack Sale, Mr Arthur Foulser and many others who helped but have not been mentioned by name.

I would also like to thank the following authors for permission to quote extracts from their books: Mr Brian Lunn, *Aircraft Down II: Air Crashes in Wharfedale & Nidderdale*, Hardwick Publications; Mr Simon Parry, *Intruders Over Britain*, Air Research Publications; Mr Gordon Ramsey, *The Blitz—Then and Now Vol 2*, After The Battle Publications; Mr John W. Gee DFC, *Wingspan: The Recollections of a Bomber Pilot*, published by the author. Mr John F. Hamlin *The Royal Air Force in Cambridge*, published by J. F. Hamlin. Mr John Hampton *A Brief History*, RAF Westcott. And my special thanks to the RAF Museum Hendon for allowing me to use their Airfield Map of Steeple Morden.

Finally, I would like to express my thanks to my wife for her support and encouragement during the past eighteen months, and for the endless cups of coffee. Thank you, Liz.

Dedication

The author wishes to dedicate this book to two people, the first, the late Frank Huffer, who lived and farmed around the airfield all his life, and who gave invaluable assistance during the research for this book, and secondly Harold Coates, Ex 11 OTU, for his copious letters of his time at Steeple Morden. Both sadly did not live to see its completion.

No.11 Operational Training Unit
Steeple_Morden

No.17 Operational Training Unit

Introduction

The number of books written about airfield histories is countless but hopefully this book tells of the men and women who were brought together in the early days of the war to serve at RAF Steeple Morden, a satellite airfield of RAF Bassingbourn, and the people in the surrounding villages who by their close proximity to the airfield were to be so involved in its history.

I hope this book will also convey the part played by the many people in Steeple Morden and surrounding villages who enrolled in the very early days of the war as ARP Wardens, Firewatchers, Special Constables or as members of the Red Cross, Land Army, Women's Voluntary Service, The Auxiliary Fire Service and the Home Guard. And finally I hope that this book will succeed in conveying the atmosphere of the time and be a memorial to the men of 11 OTU and 17 OTU (Operational Training Units) who gave their lives whilst serving at Steeple Morden and Bassingbourn.

As you drive from Steeple Morden Village on the Litlington Road it is very difficult to imagine that the vast open space on the right hand side of the road was once an aerodrome; long gone are the sounds of Wellingtons, Blenheims, Ansons, Thunderbolts and Mustangs. Only a few of the buildings and a part of the perimeter track remain, where those mighty aircraft taxied, sometimes for the last time. The site where the aerodrome was has now returned to its original use, agriculture, the only sound now to be heard being the wind blowing through the ripening corn.

It is some fifty years since the Air Ministry requisitioned the land, initially for a Royal Air Force satellite airfield, which later became a front line aerodrome for the American 355th Fighter Group. One lasting feature is the memorial to the Americans who gave their lives whilst serving at Steeple

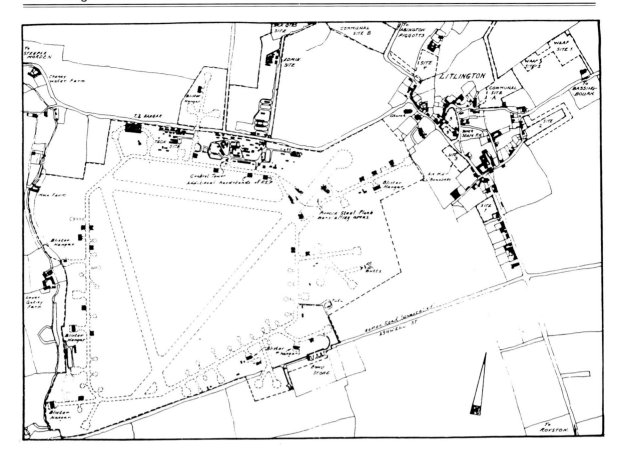

Morden, and as I write the Steeple Morden branch of the Royal British Legion have decided to erect a memorial on the airfield to the many RAF personnel who also died whilst serving with 11 and 17 OTU. It was 11 Operational Training Unit which first arrived to train, on Ansons and Wellington bombers, and later 17 OTU arrived in their Blenheims. This is their story of courage and heroism in the early days of the war.

I am indebted to the many people I have talked to, and who shared their stories and memories with me, and I hope this will stir many more, as the Second World War was for some the most powerful experience of their lives. The official information has come from The Public Records Office at Kew, and the county record offices in Cambridge and Hertford, The Royal Air Force Museum Hendon, The Imperial War Museum The Air Historical Branch (MoD) and from officers and men and women who served at Steeple Morden, together with the villagers who lived around the airfield. Sometimes their stories differ from official records, but I can only relate the stories as they were told to me.

First let us go back to 1937 when the RAF was starting to build vast new aerodromes, and Bassingbourn was ear-

marked for a major airfield while Steeple Morden was selected as its satellite. The site selected was south-east of the village on a sloping site which was not ideal by any means, but with Chamberlain's return from Munich in 1939 a war seemed a possibility so speed to build airfields in Great Britain was of the essence.

Looking towards 'Upper Gatley Farm' today only a 20ft wide strip of the perimeter track remains.

(Author)

Chapter 1
Construction of the Airfield

Chapter 1

Construction of the Airfield

At a meeting of the Steeple Morden Parish Council in December 1938 it was decided that a strongly worded letter should be sent to the Air Ministry, and to the Cambridgeshire County Council, that it totally disapproved of the 300 acres that was being proposed for requisition for the building of a new aerodrome near the village since the land was of prime agricultural use. Alas, it was to no avail and the Air Ministry insisted that the aerodrome had to be built, quoting the Defence of the Realm Act. The next thing the villagers knew was when buff Air Ministry envelopes fell through their letter boxes, informing them that their land was to be requisitioned. Three farmers lost their farms—George Jarman, George Smyth and Bert Parrish—together with many small-holdings on the Litlington Road. Once terms had been agreed (and it would seem that many farmers reached favourable terms in the early days before war was declared, while later they were not so favourable), the surveyors quickly arrived with their theodolites and took readings, and all too soon large earth moving machines and graders arrived and all the trees and hedges were removed and ditches filled in. One local farmer's son at the time, Peter Jarman, recalls it was in the middle of a harvest when the giant earth movers arrived and crushed the corn flat; no time could be spared to bring in the harvest.

John Laing and Son, who were already building Bassingbourn Airfield, were given the contract together with John Willmotts, who were responsible for building the hutted accommodation, and very soon after the initial levelling of the site, John Innes and Son's lorries (one of the main sub-contractors) started to bring in thousands of tons of ballast. One local lad, Fred Hitch, who was working as an office boy on the site, remembers the lorry drivers were on piece work, and

John Laing not only built
Steeple Morden but hundreds
of airfields in East Anglia during
the 1940's.
(John Laing Plc)

worked all hours bringing the ballast from the gravel pits in
Bedford—much to the annoyance of the villagers, as the
roads were never built to handle so much traffic. With so
many lorries being used in the construction of the airfield it
was difficult to keep a check on loads, and some of the lorry
drivers went in one entrance and out of the other, and then
straight back in again, some earning a lot of money this way.
With deadlines to be met, accidents were inevitable; one little
girl was run over and killed by a ballast lorry in Ashwell village.

Many local people thought it a strange place to build an
aerodrome as the proposed sloping site had a large hump in
the middle of it, and one could not see one side from the
other. Even after many months of levelling the hump is still
there to this day. Another problem with the site was a
wooded hillside at the south-west end of the main runway,
which was to cause some dicey take-offs. Eventually a number
of trees were felled on the top of the hill, but not before a few
aircraft had crashed into the woods. The site was bounded on
its south side by Ashwell Strete, a part of the Icknield Way—
a Roman road—which was closed to the public as the Bomb
Store was built on a part of it, plus aircraft hardstands.

Many nationalities were brought in during the airfield's
construction. There were Indians, Pakistanis and, of course,
the Irish who came in vast numbers, who could lay bricks and
pipes, and dig trenches in record time. At the end of the con-

tract one of the village girls married one of the Irish workmen and went to live in Australia.

Some of the workmen were billeted in houses around the village, others were accommodated in wooden huts on the airfield, and people still remember the strange cooking smells wafting across the fields. . .

During construction the workmen complained that they feared an attack on the airfield, so an Armadillo armoured car with twin machine-guns was brought over from Bassingbourn and parked at the end of one of the nearly completed runways, in case of a daylight air attack.

As initially the site was only for a satellite airfield, no brick buildings were constructed, just runways, a perimeter track and a few Nissen huts, plus petrol storage for 72,000 gallons of high octane fuel, and 3,500 gallons for the MT section. The runways were laid down in the standard triangular pattern. The runway lengths were NE to SW 5,000 feet; EW 3,250 feet; and NW to SE, 3,350 feet. All were 150 feet in width. It was not until 1941 that it was decided to improve the airfield and 55 concrete hardstands were provided which were later supplemented by some pierced steel plank ones. In 1943 a type T2 hangar, seven blister hangars and a watch office (control tower), were also constructed.

The dispersed living quarters were situated around Litlington village at seven sites plus two WAAF sites which,

After the surveyors had left large earth moving machines were brought in to work on runway levelling. (*John Laing Plc*)

After the initial levelling, drains were dug and thousands of tons of concrete was laid. The first runway to be completed was the No. 3 runway close to the Litlington Road. (*John Laing Plc*)

after the Americans arrived, could accommodate some 2,000 personnel. The Americans also added their own base hospital with beds for 24 patients, mortuary and ambulance station. One thing that did annoy the locals was the building of a sewage farm so that the aerodrome could be on mains drainage, but it was to be many years later that the village itself was actually put onto mains drainage.

So, with one runway nearing completion, it would not be long before the aircraft were to fly in. The initial cost of building the airfield with runways and perimeter track but with no buildings, according to the archives at Laings, was £180,674 0s 0p, a considerable sum in 1939.

The building of the aerodrome was not without accidents. Even before the aerodrome was officially opened, a Wellington bomber made an emergency landing with a full load of practice bombs and went off the edge of the grass into a ditch. Jack Sale, then a lad of sixteen, was working on the airfield at the time, and was asked to help unload the practice bombs by the pilot. Jack picked up a bomb and threw it on to the grass, thinking it was harmless. Unfortunately, it exploded, putting him in hospital with shrapnel injuries for many months, some of which are still coming to surface in his legs to this day.

Although the airfield was constructed only to last for the duration of the war, it was well made as some of the buildings

remain to this day. Three Nissen huts near the memorial were used by Americans as pilots' ready rooms, where they waited for takeoff. The brick-built building on the opposite side of the road was the operations block, where all the flight operations were planned; it also had a very early type of filtered ventilation system, some of which has survived to this day. The building closer to the road was a part of the main workshops. The bomb store was situated on the far side of the airfield on Ashwell Strete, the base of which is still there, as well as a derelict pillbox near the river at Upper Gatley Farm. Also close by is a Nissen hut which was used as a maintenance hut, but is now used for farm storage.

It was a time of great activity, but not just at Steeple Morden, as, at its height airfield, construction in Great Britain engaged some 60,000 men on some 560 airfields in the British Isles.

Searchlight sites were also being built in the area, to assist in the defence against enemy aircraft and to help aircraft lost in the forthcoming night flying operations. One man who recalls building them was Harry Hart from Guilden Morden, who remembers some of the tricks played on him and his mates by the Army detachment whilst completing the Cold Harbour site, close to the present farm shop at Beverly Farm. He says that the favourite trick of the Army Detachment was

Mr Dud Charter and Mr Quaff Wilkins taken during the construction of the airfield. (*Mrs M. Dickinson*)

All that remains of F/O R. V. Jeff's Hawker Hurricane after he parachuted to safety. The Hurricane L1618 from 87 Squadron Debden, crashed into the orchard next to the church in Steeple Morden, after he became dazzled by a searchlight in 1939. (Cambridge Collection)

to crank the searchlight level and switch it on; you could feel it burning your back, right through your overalls.

The searchlight at this site was responsible in the bringing down of a Hurricane in 1939, flown by Flight Lieutenant Robert Voase Jeff while on a night flying formation exercise with three other Hurricanes from 87 Squadron, Debden. When he was dazzled by the searchlight, fearing he might collide with the other two he decided to bale out, his Hurricane crashing near the church in Steeple Morden. That night Aubrey Wright was cycling past the church when he noticed the pilot carrying his parachute. Minutes earlier Voase Jeff had landed at the rear of the church, luckily just missing landing on the steeple. He asked Aubrey where the nearest telephone was so he could report the crash. Putting the pilot on the saddle, Aubrey pedalled as fast as he could to the nearest telephone. Leaving the pilot, he returned to the crash site to warn the gathering crowd, as by now ammunition from the Hurricane was exploding in the flames.

Flight Lieutenant Voase Jeff later went to France and shot down the first German Heinkel 111 to crash on French soil, for which he was awarded the Croix de Guerre. On returning to England, he fought throughout the early part of the Battle of Britain, acquiring the DFC and Bar. On 11 August 1940 he was last seen diving on an enemy aircraft over the Channel. In 1990 some of the remains of his Mk I Hurricane, serial number *L1618*, were found at the crash site in Steeple Morden, together with a part of the Watts wooden propeller blade.

Steeple Morden church today. In 1939 Flight Lieutenant Voase Jeff landed by parachute just left of the steeple.

(*Author*)

Facing page:
Searchlight similar to the one used at the Cold Harbour site, Steeple Morden.

STEEPLE MORDEN

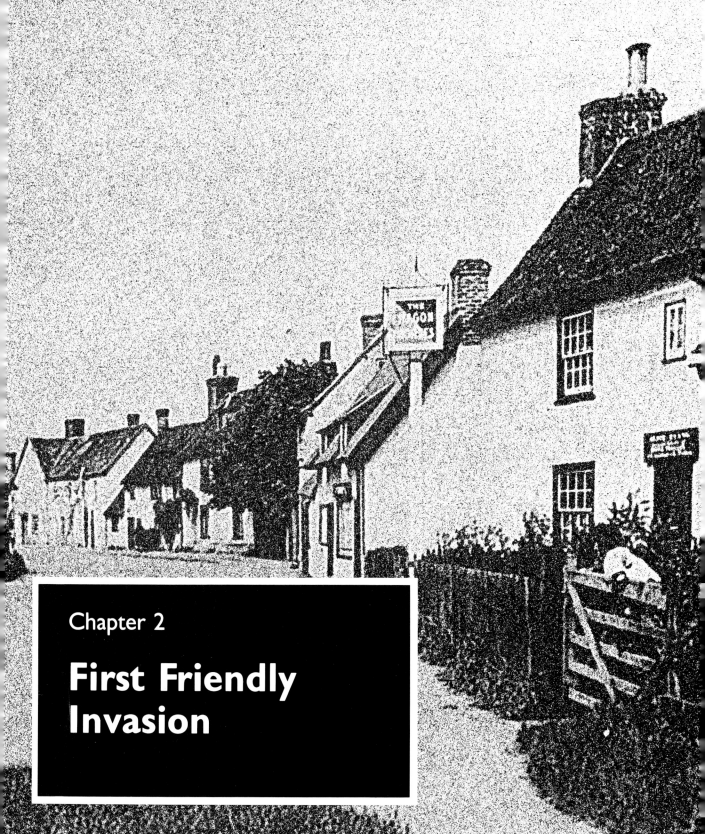

Chapter 2

First Friendly Invasion

Chapter 2

First Friendly Invasion

With the aerodrome nearing completion, the RAF was concerned with the accommodation for the crews and ground crews. The villagers of Steeple Morden and Litlington were asked to accommodate the personnel soon to arrive. Some were billeted in local homes, the unfortunate ones sleeping under canvas in old 'Bell' type tents in the grounds of Kneesworth Hall and surrounding sites.

One airman who remembers his billet is Jim Sharp, who recalls it as being a small room with no heating, just a bed and two blankets and hardly any other furniture. Sharing the room was another chap from Birmingham, who snored with a Brummey accent. His second billet was a bungalow where the

Hay Street, Steeple Morden.

landlady was very houseproud and made them take their shoes off at the front door. This was really comfortable, but due to illness Sharp had to move on yet again. The third move was back to basics again. Unfortunately this move led to him being put on a charge: coming home late from the 'Waggon and Horses' he found himself locked out and attempted to get in through an upstairs window, but stepping on a not so secure shelf he fell off and woke up the whole household.

Harold Coates has more happy memories of his billet with Mr and Mrs Ball and their two teenage daughters Doris and Mary in Litlington. The cottage had no running water or electricity, only an outside water butt for washing in, which in the winter froze over, but it was wonderful as the family made his two mates and himself feel at home and a part of the family.

The old Steeple Morden telephone exchange, the home of Lily and Harriet Matthews, was also used as a billet, with two airmen in the attic and eight in the house. John Savage recalls that these airmen were constantly being told to keep the noise from their gramophone down as Miss Matthews couldn't hear the telephone ringing at the switchboard. But probably the most sought after billet was 'The Crown' pub at Litlington. Jim Powling recalls there was no drinking after hours, but did enjoy his six-month stay. His next move was to the home of Mrs Marjorie Pearce, and finally to the Post Office in Litlington run by Mr Reg Allan and his daughter Sheila (the sub post-mistress), who recalls that men billeted with them and in Litlington gave no trouble and were welcomed by the villagers. With most of the billets nearing completion

'The Crown' Litlington.

'Then and Now'
Jim Powling second from the
left, outside this billet at Sharp's
Farm, Litlington.
B Flight:
Jeff Whittle, Jim Powling,
Frank Mabon, Peter Rayford,
Paddy Herrow, Jock Caincross,
—? Hooper.

Jim Powling when he revisited
the site in 1990.
(*J. Powling and author*)

Jim Powling was moved to his new billet at Sharp's Farm,
Litlington. Even the Rectory (now the Old Rectory) had two
airmen billeted on them, one of them a squadron leader. With
the Rectory being right on the edge of the airfield at the end
of the main runway, the squadron leader was able to keep an
eye on what was going on.

A house requisitioned was 'Lilton House'; this was the
farm house of Mr and Mrs George Jarman on whose land a
part of the airfield was built. The Jarman family being moved
into a bungalow further down the road, they also had two airmen billeted on them. Billeted in the farm house was a Pilot

Litlington village, the old Post Office is on the left, where many airmen were billeted, including Jim Powling. (*Sheila Allen*)

Instructor whose Wellington was kept on a hardstand virtually in the farm's back-garden, much to the delight of Mr and Mrs Jarman's two sons, Peter and Ken, who, when nobody was around, were allowed to clamber inside and play.

Now that most of the personnel had been found accommodation training could start and the villages of Steeple Morden and Litlington would vibrate to the sound of aeroplane engines for many years to come. But soon there was to be a new influx of faces, as the village was about to get evacuees from Islington, North London. They arrived in two red double decker buses with a teacher, clutching a small case or bag in one hand and round their necks they carried their gas masks in cardboard boxes. For most of them it was their first time away from home, and one villager recalls they all looked tired, hungry and dirty. When one of them was given a bath he shouted out 'Don't drown me, mister'. Fifty-five children arrived initially, followed in 1941 by 33 London policemen's wives and their children. With so many children in the village one of the local doctors, Sheila Moynihan, decided to start a clinic, which was held in the home of Mrs Rigg who lived in 'Two Trees' in Hay Street and was staffed by members of the Red Cross. It came to be known as the 'Felicity Mary Clinic'.

The villages of South Cambridgeshire were asked to

Lily Willmott in her Land Army uniform. (*Lily Willmott*)

A Land Army Girl in uniform whilst on a visit to Guilden Morden. Circa 1943. (*John Deller*)

accommodate some 6,000 children at the outbreak of war, but by January 1940 many had returned home, only to return when the bombing started.

With so many men from villages all over the country being called up for military service, women were being called upon to work on the land, and join the Women's Land Army. They were not, strictly speaking, an army in the military sense, but joined up to do battle with the land and livestock. Their uniform consisted of corduroy breeches, green jumper, brown jacket and a khaki broad brimmed hat, which became a familiar sight on farms all over the country. Initially the Land Army was voluntary but by 1943 it was almost impossible for women to avoid some kind of war work. Many farms in the surrounding areas soon had women doing jobs that had pre-

LAC Lionel Hughes was billeted here with Mrs Carlow at 'Swadlincote', Litlington.

Leading Aircraftsman Lionel Hughes in 1940.

viously been carried out by men. Some found the work very hard, especially if they arrived at harvest time. Many of the girls adapted readily to the work but some were so unhappy they returned home.

The pay was very poor, £1 8s 0d for a fifty-hour week, out of which they had to pay for their lodgings. By June 1944 the Land Army totalled some 80,000 members. One of the girls was Lily Wilmott (née Atherton), who came to Morden Heath Farm from Manchester and ended up marrying a local man, as did many other girls. Lily still remembers with affection the Land Army motto 'Stick to it', and stick to it they did and the farms all over Cambridgeshire and England were all the better for their valuable assistance.

One of the first aircraft to make a landing on the still unfinished aerodrome was a Fairey Battle watched by the young Don Hitch and his mates from the school playground. After school they went up to the airfield and watched the Fairey Battle having some work done on its engine. One of

B. Flight out for a ride at Steeple
Morden. Where are they now?
(L. Hughes)

the mechanics called them over, and asked them if they
would like to sit on the tail while they taxied it across the airfield, much to the delight of the youngsters. The following
day it flew off, but not before giving the kids a couple of low
passes over the school.

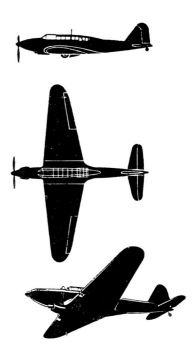

Chapter 3

Training Commences

Chapter 3

Training Commences

With the airfield still not quite completed, 8 April 1940 was an important day as Bomber Command began forming their Operational Training Units. Bassingbourn, still a group training pool, was renumbered 11 OTU and on 17 April, 215 Squadron was absorbed into it together with its 54 Wellington 1s, 1as and 1cs, 11 Ansons and later two Lysanders for target towing. In May a further 11 Wellingtons arrived to swell the strength. Five flights operated from Bassingbourn and Steeple

Wellington Mk I's as used by 11 OTU on a training exercise. (MOD)

Westland Lysander of the type used at Bassingbourn for target towing, this one is from the 1483 (Target Towing) Flight based at Newmarket. (*Tim Holden*)

Morden, 'A' and 'C' and 'E' from Bassingbourn, 'B', 'D' from Steeple Morden. A total of one hundred aircraft served with the unit, spread between the two airfields. Avro Ansons were used for cross country navigation and wireless transmission training. As Steeple Morden was to undertake a considerable amount of flying, a maintenance flight was moved over from Bassingbourn.

The main use for the satellite was for circuit flying and training and secondly for the dispersal of aircraft in case of air attack. Early on in the war, due to the urgent need for bomber crews, the training was cut fairly short. On average flying crews spent between four and eight weeks at an OTU where they were crewed up and trained on the type of aircraft they would fly in at an operational squadron; with weather permitting, they flew night and day. The instructors found that training aircrew was more hazardous than flying on operations, and was certainly no rest-cure, as many of them had not even had the opportunity to take an instructor's course. Having graduated from Tiger Moths, Harvards and Oxfords, the trainee pilots discovered that the Wellington was not an easy aeroplane to fly at first, finding the conversion to over ten tons of aircraft, two 1,050-horsepower engines, and a wingspan of over 86 feet a challenge, but eventually they got

R.A.F. BASSINGBOURNE
— No. 11 O.T.U —
— STAFF OBSERVERS —

Sgt. BRADFORD | Sgt. HIGGY | Sgt. CONWAY | Sgt. SMITH D.F.M | Sgt. BARRAND | Sgt. JAMES

Sgt. WHEATLEY | Sgt. ANSTEY D.F.M | Sgt. JONES | Sgt. GRIFFITH | Sgt. MYLE | Sgt. ORCHARD | Sgt. SCOUT

II OTU Sergeant Staff Observers at Bassingbourn. (S. Conway)

to love it, and its geodetic construction could take a lot of punishment from the heavy-handed trainee pilots. To start with they would do a few take-offs and landings with an instructor flying the aircraft, then they would try it themselves with an instructor sitting in as the second pilot and finally, they would go 'solo', a great thrill. Then more circuits and bumps, initially in daylight, then at night, followed by ground training lectures in engine handling, theory of bombing, dinghy drill, meteorology and finally fighter evasion.

The air observer responsible for the navigation and bomb aiming arrived at the OTU having only completed some 30 hours' solo navigation—and all in daylight. He soon found out that navigating at night under black-out conditions was not easy, and often relied on the crew to assist him, especially the gunners front and rear who, sometimes without realising it, helped the lost navigator by unwittingly mentioning some landmark. On one occasion a navigator, totally lost on a cross-country exercise, passed a note to that effect to the pilot; the captain then decided to land at the nearest aerodrome he could find and, having found out where they were, took off again without the rest of the crew realising why they had landed.

The final training of wireless operator/air gunners was

Facing page:
'Where are they now?' This photograph was given to Mrs Doris Foster, ex-landlady of the 'Angel' public house in Royston which was frequented by many RAF personnel from II OTU. The 'Angel' pub has also disappeared. (*Mrs D. Foster*)

No. 27. A.Gs. COURSE. (3 SQUADS)
TOP ROW: A.G. CROOK. FOXON. SHIPLEY. GREEN. STANFORD. TURNER. CULLEN. WAKEFIELD. STONE. BRAGAN. ANDREWS.
MIDDLE ROW:- A.G. QUINN. A/F/C: THOM. STORRY. DALTON. JONES. THOMSON. THORLEY. CRABB. A/C: DAVIS. HIBBERT.
BOTTOM ROW:- A/G. BLATCHLEY. SMITH. CHEEK. MILLER. BINNS. MITCHELL. JOHNSON. GAMBLE. PAUL.

No. 27 Air Gunners course at Manby, prior to coming to Bassingbourn. (*G. F. Stanford*)

carried out at Bassingbourn in classrooms divided into cubicles simulating aircraft installations, using pre-war R1082/T1083 receiver/transmitter radios for instruction and practice. Later more up-to-date Marconi T1154/R1155 were used. The next part of the training was to fly in Avro Ansons, when several wireless operators took it in turns to practice air-to-ground transmissions.

The airgunners' operational training consisted of firing at drogues towed at Bassingbourn by Westland Lysanders, and at ground targets. They also trained on the machine gun range. The Wellington MK.1C armament consisted of a power operated rear turret housing two .303 machine guns, and a further two in the nose plus two .303 beam-mounted machine guns. The intensity of the gunners' training is given in the Operations Record Book that in July 1942 the gunners fired; 148,700 rounds of ammunition at air to air targets, 7,600 rounds at targets on the ground, and 400 rounds on operations.

As with most OTU the crewing up procedure was left to natural selection, among the crews themselves, and would consist of a Pilot, Navigator, Bomb Aimer, Wireless Operator/ Air Gunner, and Rear Gunner. With most of them newly qualified, they carried the rank of sergeant, with a small number promoted at the end of their basic flying training to the rank of Pilot Officer or Flying Officer. Some were OTU instructors preparing to do a second tour, from their so called 'rest'.

In the early days there were many accidents. At Bassingbourn they lost 20 Wellingtons in a matter of days. At Steeple Morden, with one of the runways still under construction, a steamroller was being used near the end of the main runway. A Wellington with a trainee crew aboard failed to gain sufficient height on take-off, and its undercarriage struck the steamroller near its chimney. The massive roller almost disintegrated, with the driver being thrown out and seriously injured. The Wellington just managed to get airborne, and circled the airfield several times until it was ascertained that the damage appeared to be confined to one burst main wheel attached to a useless dangling oleo leg. The pilot eventually landed on one wheel, doing only slight damage to the aircraft; the crew were a bit shaken up but escaped without injury.

On another occasion, a pilot on his first solo flight attempted to land a Wellington with the undercarriage still retracted (which was to become a regular occurrence at Steeple Morden). Despite the warning klaxon sounding in the cockpit, which everybody else could hear, the Wellington just

Ian Adams (ground crew) standing in front of a MkI Wellington L4304. (OP-J) at Steeple Morden. His wife's name Doreen is chalked on the side. (*H. Coates*)

slid along the runway. The pilot later said he was concentrating so hard on landing that he never heard it. Luckily the damage to the aircraft was minimal and it was soon flying again.

Not all pilots had such lucky escapes. One trainee pilot attempted to take off with his propellers in the wrong pitch, with a consequent loss of power. The pilot attempted to correct his mistake, but he had left it too late, and with the aircraft barely airborne it struck the top of a parked Wellington and burst into flames, crashing on the boundary of the airfield. Only one member of the crew managed to escape, the others dying in the inferno.

A week later a brand new Wellington was delivered to Bassingbourn from a maintenance unit, but it was decided to move it to Steeple Morden. This particular aircraft was named 'City of Birmingham' as it had been paid for by the people of Birmingham, but coming in to land on a shortened runway due to building work it overshot and crashed into some earth works and was a total write-off, after having flown for only five hours. Luckily the crew escaped without injury.

As well as doing circuits and bumps the trainee pilots had to practice 'overshoot procedure', in which they had to come

'B' Flight, Steeple Morden 1940. (*H. Coates*)

in to land with the undercarriage down and full flap. At a given command by the instructor, they had to open up the throttles, raise the undercarriage and flaps. Unfortunately the undercarriage control and the flap control were side by side and many a confused young pilot whipped up both controls almost together and the poor old 'Wimpy' just fell out of the sky. The correct procedure was to whip the undercarriage control up quickly, but the flaps had to be bled off very slowly indeed to allow the aircraft to gain more airspeed and thus more lift.

When the fault and the cause of the accidents became known the controls were modified so the hydraulic lever on the valve could be pushed down to its full travel, while the return movement to raise the flaps could only be moved slightly upwards, opening the valve a very small amount, thus raising the flaps very slowly. It was a very successful 'mod', reducing the number of 'overshoot' accidents and saving many lives.

Another problem that faced the trainee pilots was the difficulty of maintaining control in the event of an engine failure or losing power. Many inexperienced pilots would instinctively open up the throttle of the good engine to increase power and

A Wellington at Bassingbourn having come to grief after its port tyre burst on landing, during a training flight. (*W. Craigen*)

Above:
Ground crew enjoying the summer sun outside one of the huts which were located next to the Litlington Road, Steeple Morden. (*G. Tyack*)

Centre picture:
'Out for a ride' Steeple Morden Airfield. L/R Claydon, Powling, Fitz-Hugh, Verdon, Manderson, Familton. (*H. Coates*)

pull back the control column to try to maintain height and at the same time attempt to land. This usually met with disastrous results. Experience taught them that when this happened you had to throttle back the good engine, and ease the control column forward to lower the nose, letting the aircraft increase speed until it was higher than the critical speed then, gradually increase the power on the good engine; this was, of course, assuming that you had plenty of height. It was said that if you survived the OTU course you were very likely to survive your tour of operations.

With training going on night and day the ground crews were kept very busy as the aircraft were flying some 18 hours a day. Servicing was carried out in the open, no mean task in the middle of winter, when the ground crews were often wet through, suffering from frozen fingers, and having to work by torchlight. Steeple Morden was thought by one corporal fitter to be the coldest, muddiest and windiest airfield he ever had the pleasure to work on. The ground crews found the Pegasus XVIII engine on the Wellingtons to be relatively easy to work on, even though it suffered from high oil consumption, and numerous oil leaks which meant continual cleaning of the nacelles and wings.

The servicing of 'B' Flight aircraft was under 'Chiefy', Flight Sergeant Pike, and Sergeants Thompson and 'Sandy'

II OTU 'B' Flight Steeple Morden sitting on a 'Bowser' June 1941. L/R Collins, Familton, Adams, Claydon, Caird, Powling, Manderson, Verdon, and Cpl. Irving. (*H. Coates*)

Sanderson, who, together with seven fitters and several riggers, stayed together from 1940 to 1942. 'D' Flight aircraft were under the ever watchful eye of Flight Sergeant Crabb, who by all accounts allowed his flight a tot of rum to keep out the cold. They worked a weekly rota, with a change-over from days to nights each Friday. When changing to night work they worked from 8 am Friday to 8 am Saturday. The night flying party worked 5 pm to 8 am daily until the following Friday 8 am, and then had 24 hours off. The daytime party worked 8 am to 5 pm. Breakfast was at 7 am and tea at 5 pm, while the night flying party had supper (the main meal) at 11 pm or midnight unless the night flying was cancelled.

Food at first was brought over from Bassingbourn in hay boxes, cooked in a makeshift field kitchen and eaten in a marquee, but a few of the ground crew preferred to have a snack in the builders' canteen, which was run by a father and daughter who was nicknamed 'Dirty Mary' but who by all accounts made smashing bacon rolls. Eventually the ground crews were barred, as it was said they were stealing civilian rations. Later proper dining huts were built, but the most welcome sight was the NAAFI or WVS van touring the dispersals. The same marquee which was used as a mess was also used initially as the Crew Room and the Flight Office and by all accounts was very cold, drafty and extremely muddy, as

Wellington MkI L4387 (LG-L) joined 11 OTU in April 1940, and crashed on take-off from Bassingbourn 31.8.40, killing its crew of six. (*Tower Museum, Bassingbourn*)

Can you remember 'Amy' who worked in the NAAFI at Bassingbourn or Steeple Morden? (*G. Taylor*)

was the airfield. The trainee pilots soon discovered not to taxi off the runway or they would get stuck in the mud, which would then mean a tractor was needed to pull them out, hence Steeple Morden became affectionately known as 'Steeple Bollock'.

There were all nationalities under training at Steeple Morden, especially New Zealanders, as well as Poles, Czechs, Australians, Canadians and Indians. Most of the aircrew trainees who trained at 11 OTU were wartime volunteers, as were the instructors. In fact only a small percentage of all the air crew in Bomber Command in World War Two were regular members of the RAF. The age limits for aircrew were between 18–32 but, later in the war with mounting losses, youths of 17½ were accepted for training. Although New Zealanders formed only a small part of Bomber Command, many of them did their operational training at No 11 OTU which is perpetuated in the unit's badge which includes two Maori spears in saltire; the six annulets conjoined is indicative of the strength of the aircrews united in the cause of their training. It is interesting to note that the only Victoria Cross awarded to a member of a Wellington crew was a New Zealander, a Sergeant J. A. Ward, RNZAF, who received his award in 1941.

Although there were many pubs in the two villages, the

nearest pub to the airfield was 'The Fox', which with the arrival of very thirsty men would often run dry as beer and spirits were in short supply during the war. A barmaid at the time, Avis Brocket remembers the Indians coming into the pub wearing their turbans, much to the amusement of the locals.

Jim Sharp, who joined the RAF in 1940 and was posted to 11 OTU at Bassingbourn/Steeple Morden, recalls in those early days that if you put your hands in your pocket for your handkerchief they would have you on a charge. His first job was in the ACC (accumulator room), charging batteries, and this produced many amusing memories; for example, so that he and his friends could acquire new tunics, he gave a little bit of extra fair wear and tear to their old ones using battery acid. . .

Shortly after his arrival at Bassingbourn Jim remembers a sign beside a large bomb crater near the main gate saying 'Thank you'. This was not from a German bomb, but from a British Whitley bomber from 10 Squadron based at Dishforth in Yorkshire. The crew thought they were over Germany, having mistaken the Thames Estuary for the Rhine due to high winds and heavy cloud. Bassingbourn had a lucky escape that night as the stick of ten bombs narrowly missed the main bomb dump. The following day the red-faced pilot was made to personally apologise to the Bassingbourn CO. But the story does not end there for the following week a Spitfire based at nearby Duxford dropped five 'Iron Crosses' over the bomber's base at Dishforth.

Another near miss was when Jim Sharp was in the Watch Office at Steeple Morden with Sergeants Bond and Tattershal. Night flying was in operation and the three of them were standing just outside the Watch Office when, suddenly, they heard the whistling of a bomb. Throwing themselves on the ground, they heard it land a short distance away but fortunately fail to explode. Jim thought his name was on that one!

About a week later, two pilots were carrying out their first night solo flight when a Jerry intruder joined the circuit and shot them down. Some instructor pilots raced to a spare aircraft and took off in the hope of shooting down the German, while the rest of the ground crew boarded what vehicles they could and raced across the aerodrome to the crash, expecting the worst. When they arrived at the crashed Wellington they found both pilots sitting near the wreckage waiting for someone to light up a cigarette for them.

Sometimes the intruders arrived without any warning, as one instructor recalls. 'I had just lined up on the runway for take-off when a stick of bombs exploded right down the flarepath ahead of me, causing my aircraft to jump with each explosion and ending up 90 degrees to the runway.' On

Mr G. Taylor with one of the cooks at Steeple Morden in 1942. (*G. Taylor*)

Jim Sharp II OTU November 1940. (*J. Sharp*)

another occasion two pupils on their night solo were shot down as they turned on to their Finals for landing, their aircraft descending very slowly in flames. The crash crew on arrival could find no trace of them, but an hour or so later they turned up at the Flight Office. Apparently the aircraft had literally floated down to earth on fire and landed intact with the pilots uninjured. They had walked back across the fields to the airfield. Later that morning, after a medical check-up they were flying again.

As so many aircraft were now being attacked it was decided that all aircraft would carry a tail gunner on all training flights. This did not go down well with the tail gunners as it was bad enough being in this hazardous position, but flying with a trainee pilot, doing circuits and bumps, was thought to be suicidal.

One night an instructor with a pupil pilot was in the circuit waiting to land when, suddenly, the landing lights below were extinguished and Very light signals from the ground indicated that a German intruder was in the circuit. The pilot immediately called on the intercom to the tail gunner to keep his eyes peeled, and put on his navigation lights, with the intention of drawing the enemy's fire and shooting it down. In due course a message was received that it was OK to land as the intruder had left the circuit. After they had landed the instructor and pupil went off for a cup of tea, telling the rear gunner to join them. When he never arrived at the tea-van they went back to the Wellington and found, to their horror, that the gunner was not in the aircraft, and the rear turret was broadside on to the fuselage. Hours later the rear gunner walked through the main gate carrying his parachute, having misunderstood the instructor. Just catching the words 'enemy aircraft . . . fire. . .' he had baled out. . .

Mk IAs in 1940. These Wellingtons still in the squadron codes of 215 Squadron, although they had been absorbed into II OTU. (Mr M. J. Bowyer)

Some of the crashes during training were due to pilot error, but one crash witnessed by Jim Sharp and his friend as they cycled to Baldock still has them wondering if it was pilot error or a malfunction with the aircraft. Jim takes up the story. 'As we got to the top of the hill out of Ashwell village we saw a Wellington flying first nose heavy, then nose up. Eventually it went into a long and laborious spin. We both pedalled and ran like hell across the fields to where the aircraft had crashed. On arriving at the scene the aircraft was ablaze with ammunition exploding. We first went to the cockpit and saw a figure in a flying jacket and at that moment he looked OK., Jim then got hold of his arm to pull him out and his arm came off in Jim's hand. Two of the dead airmen were trainee air gunners while the pilot, Flight Lieutenant Riddlesworth, was a very experienced pilot and who had already earned the DFC for flying in raids to Kiel and Stavanger. At a later court of inquiry into the crash of Wellington *L4276* at Newnham, it was stated that the Wellington stalled on recovery from an involuntary spin probably due to tail trimmers being used to recover and not being centralised before the engines were opened up. At the time there was rumour that the aircraft had been tampered with, but this was never proven.

Another one of those inexplicable crashes occurred one lovely summer's afternoon when Harold Coates and a friend were given permission to go on a two-hour 'flip' with a very experienced instructor and his two pupils. Just as they were about to take off, three ground defence boys turned up and asked the instructor if they could join in. The instructor refused to take five passengers, so as we had plenty of chances to fly, we let them go, one of the gunners being sent off to find a parachute. By the time he returned it was too late and the Wellington was already taxying out. The trio stood and watched it take off, and practice how to get out of a stall. After stalling and pulling out a few times, it went into another stall, plummeted into the ground and exploded. It was obvious that there would be no survivors. The young gunner was grief-stricken, saying that the three of them had joined up together and were inseparable until that day.

An astonishing sequel came 24 hours later, when the aerodrome came under attack during the night and the ground defences were put into action. The following morning whilst the guns were being cleaned, one accidentally went off and killed the young gunner who had cheated death the previous day.

A substantial amount of the flying from Steeple Morden was done at night with the pupil pilots doing circuits and bumps, not easy when all you had to guide you down to the

Aircrew from 215 Squadron, which later merged to become II OTU, standing by Wellington Ia *N2912* at Bassingbourn. On the night of 24.4.41., it was shot down by a Ju88 intruder and crashed onto *R1404* at its dispersal. (*Tower Museum, Bassingbourn*)

edge of the runway were gooseneck flares and a Chance light situated at the end of the runway. Once circuits and bumps were mastered the training consisted of long-distance cross-country flights at night. These were exacting tasks for the navigators and crews as there were always stories of aircraft flying into heavily defended areas, and narrowly missing the balloon barrages.

One way of assisting aircraft back to the airfield was a flashing beacon, as Corporal Sid Andrews recalls. 'We towed the beacon to various locations and set it up. When we received a wireless message that an aircraft was lost, we would then contact it with an Aldis lamp. When we got the right code of the day, we would switch on the beacon and then the airfield would light its flarepath, much to the relief of the trainee pilot.' The flashing beacon also attracted enemy aircraft. On one occasion when the beacon was parked on the roadside at the top of Orwell Hill, a German Bomber dropped a stick of bombs, the bombs falling on the grass verge narrowly missing the beacon and wireless truck.

Night landings nevertheless led to many accidents. One night a Wellington mistook the road past the airfield for the runway, crashed and was burnt out. With so many crashes the trainee crews were starting to get nervous, taking extra time doing their pre-flight checks, and sometimes trying hard to find things wrong: the flaps didn't come down right; too big a drop in revs when testing the magnetos; not enough brake pressure. The strain on these young lads was beginning to tell. The accident rate at Operational Training Units was appalling, as many as 25 per cent were lost before completing their courses: 5,327 officers and men were killed, and a further 3,113 were injured in training with Bomber Command. The most likely cause of accidents was inexperience and extremely short training in the early days of the war.

The daytime flying from Steeple Morden was for pilots going solo and for air tests. Another part of the training for the more experienced crews was 'Nickeling' (propaganda leaflet dropping) over enemy territory, an exercise which many agreed later with Air Chief Marshal Sir Arthur Harris had done no more than 'provide the enemy with five years' free supply of lavatory paper'.

Many of the Wellingtons at Steeple Morden were old Mk 1s. One in particular, *L4222*, was purported to be a jinx aircraft, recalls Harold Coates. 'This old survivor from 215 Squadron gave endless trouble to the groundcrews; as one fault was cleared another developed, and crews didn't want to fly in her. One day, after a short air test, it force landed in the middle of the aerodrome with its port engine on fire, the crew jumping out to safety when someone shouted out "Let the poor sod burn". And they did.'

At Bassingbourn and Steeple Morden training was in full swing with the more experienced crews doing 'Nickel'

Photo taken through a toilet window at Bassingbourn, as photography at RAF stations was forbidden. (J. *Powling*)

dropping in the Dunkirk, Lille, Amiens and Abbeville areas, but on 13 August a Wellington, *L4387*, taking off from Bassingbourn on a training flight at night crashed killing all the crew; Flying Officer F.A.H. Lambert (pilot), Sergeant D. O. Rewa (air observer), Sergeant H. H. Boulter (pilot), Sergeant P. Pryke (pilot), Sergeant S. Robinson (wireless operator air gunner, and Sergeant D. L. Jones (wireless operator air gunner. Eleven days later Wellington *N2945*, taking six air gunners to Jurby in the Isle of Man, crashed into the sea off Bradda Head, killing all on board.

In the village the newly formed LDV were busy collecting farm implements to use as barricades at all the entrance roads in case of an invasion. Previously all the signposts had been removed; this was intended to confuse an invading army, but their absence hindered army convoys passing through the village, as well as confusing innocent people lost in an unfamiliar village.

With the brunt of the Battle of Britain now being born by Fighter Command, the Airfields at nearby Duxford, Fowlmere and Debden came under attack. During one attack a Spitfire landed at Steeple Morden after a dog fight, out of fuel, and was refuelled with 100 octane fuel from four-gallon cans, as the bowsers only had 87 octane fuel for Wellingtons. The pilot, who was also very hungry, ate two large jam sandwiches before rejoining the battle.

At Bassingbourn two Wellingtons were being converted to counter the invasion threat. Large tanks were being fitted into their bomb bays which would be filled with hundreds of gallons of petrol. Pipes with large spreaders on the end would spray the invasion beaches, and at the same time the rear gunner would set them alight with incendiary bullets. Fortunately, this improvisation was never used.

September 1940 was the month when an invasion seemed most likely. The Home Guard was put on alert, and everybody in England waited. At the aerodrome the threat of an imminent invasion was taken seriously, all leave was cancelled and those on leave were recalled. Everyone was then confined to the aerodrome and put on stand-by. All the serviceable aircraft were got ready for immediate take off and bombed up. When the bombs ran out, the bomb bays were filled with scrap metal. The ground crews were issued old Lee-Enfield rifles and five rounds of ammunition. But, after 72 hours the threat of invasion receded and they were told to stand-down.

Saturday, 7 September 1940, was a night many people in Steeple Morden village still remember. As night fell the sky to the east of the village was a red glow. It was the London Docks receiving their first big air raid, and many villagers thought it would be their turn next as there was an aerodrome in the village.

Mr R. G. Smith taken in 1940 while at Steeple Morden. (*Mr R. G. Smith*)

It was just over two months later, on 14/15 November 1940, that Lew Hitch remembers that from early evening and for many hours he heard the distinctive sound of German aircraft engines flying in a north-westerly direction over the village, the aircraft contrails being visible in the moonlight sky.

At the airfield Corporal Sid Andrews was told to switch on his mobile flashing beacon, and he recalls that German aircraft buzzed around it all night. At approximately 10.30 pm the first recorded bombing incident took place at Steeple Morden airfield when three bombs were dropped, one failing to explode, causing no damage or injuries. It was the following day that news broadcasts revealed that Coventry had been bombed. Corporal Andrews often wondered if that was why he was told to leave the light flashing; was it to cause a diversion?

The following day three village boys, Lew Hitch, Doug Hart and Frank Oysten, decided to cycle to Royston. When they got to the level crossing outside Litlington they noticed an object in the field. Leaving Frank to look after their bikes, the other two walked over for a closer look at the 'object' which had a parachute attached to it.

Doug and Lew decided that they would like a souvenir, so with the help of a tyre lever they undid one of the nuts from the casing—not realising it was an unexploded land mine. The following day a Naval Bomb Disposal Squad blew up the land mine as it was too dangerous to move, blowing slates off nearby cottages and damaging windows. Lew and Doug still have their mementoes today, but now realise how foolish they were.

The training at 11 OTU was marred at the end of 1940 by a fatal crash when Wellington *N3014* stalled after over-shooting and crashed adjacent to Bassingbourn village killing the crew of six, Pilot Officer D.R.F. Haviland (pilot), Sergeant W. L. Jones (pilot), Pilot Officer Pennymore (observer), Sergeant B. Q. Sheppard (wireless operator/air gunner), Sergeant E. J. Peters (air gunner), and Sergeant J. A. Carrol (wireless operator/air gunner). But despite all the air raids and accidents, five pilots, eight observers, 16 wireless operator/air gunners and 16 air gunners were posted to squadrons as fully trained.

January 1941 saw Steeple Morden have an unusual visitor when a Whitley bomber, *P5060*, made an emergency landing due to bad weather after attacking the dockyards at Bremen.

Chapter 4

The Enemy Drops In

Chapter 4

The Enemy Drops In

On 16 February at approximately 4.25 am, with night flying in operation, the officer in charge of the night flying, Flight Lieutenant Bill Craigen, received a phone call from Bassingbourn. Area Fighter Control at Duxford had telephoned to say that an unidentified aircraft had entered the zone, and appeared to be heading for Steeple Morden, and a Hurricane night fighter was being vectored to intercept it. The message was passed to the flarepath and the Armadillo to keep an eye out for the suspected enemy aircraft. All of a sudden the air raid siren sounded and all the airfield lights were extinguished. The unidentified aircraft appeared in the circuit. When challenged with the colours of the day, a double red Very light, the Hurricane following it replied correctly. The

Ju88 A-5 (6214) being dismantled at Steeple Morden, prior to being moved to Farnborough for investigation. Parts of this aircraft were eventually used to keep the RAF's enemy aircraft flight flying.
(W. Craigen)

now identified German aircraft tried to escape by firing off two single red flares very quickly. The Armadillo crew, realising by now it was a German Ju88, fired off a couple of rounds from their twin Lewis machine-guns, missing the Ju88 but hitting a parked Wellington in the tail. The order was then given to cease fire, and the German aircraft was given a green signal with an Aldis lamp denoting permission to land. The Ju88 continued to circle, putting on its navigation lights, then came in to land cross-wind, across the flarepath. As it touched down one wheel dropped into a deep trench, left by some workmen who were installing 'Drem' airfield lighting. The Ju88 damaged its starboard undercarriage and propeller as it slewed across the grass for a further one hundred yards before coming to rest on its starboard wingtip.

The first person to witness the crash landing was one of Steeple Morden's special constables, John Savage, who was on patrol on Ashwell Strete. Thinking it was a Wellington bomber crashing, he ran towards the aircraft which by now had come to rest beside the hedge in the strete. To his horror he saw the swastika on the tail and decided to make a hasty retreat. Flight Lieutenant Bill Craigen, seeing the German aircraft landing, raced across the airfield in his car and clambered onto the wing. He covered the crew with a Browning automatic as they climbed out. Moments later the Armadillo and the crash tender arrived, the spotlight from the tender illuminating the fuselage from which the crew were clambering. The Germans were very quickly disarmed, even of a Very light pistol which could have been used to destroy the aircraft.

Before being taken away, the pilot asked if he could look over his aircraft. Walking to the rear he swore very loudly in

Exterior of the Ju88. Note the hastily blacked out insignia on the tail and fuselage.
(*W. Craigan*)

Pilot Officer Boggis looking out of the captured Ju88 A-5 (6214) at Steeple Morden. (*W. Craigen*)

German, as he realised the damage to the tail, which was causing the Ju88 to judder, was minor, and that they could have made it back home after all. Jim Powling recalls that when the pilot took off his flying overalls he had an immaculate Luftwaffe uniform and was carrying a small attaché case which contained a toothbrush and pyjamas. (Jim tried to negotiate with the pilot to exchange caps, but the German officer refused.) The other members of the crew were all scruffy and dirty, one of them trembling with fear, as he thought he was about to be shot. The four prisoners were put in the Armadillo and taken to Bassingbourn for interrogation. The driver recalls that the pilot was very arrogant, and said 'You will never win this war', in excellent English. The driver's reply was in the traditional RAF manner! With the prisoners safely on their way, Flight Lieutenant Craigen telephoned Bassingbourn operations room to report the incident. The Senior Duty Operations Officer, Squadron Leader Jock du Boulay's reply was, 'Craigen, it's very late and this is no time of the morning to be playing silly jokes—and get on with the night flying'. I understand his face was a picture when the prisoners arrived.

On arrival at Bassingbourn the pilot was placed under guard in the Ladies' Room, while the other members of the crew were taken to the Guard Room, where they proved to be very truculent and refused to eat for several days.

Interior shots of the Ju88 A-5 (Werke Nr 1625). These photographs were taken in great secrecy the following morning after the crash by Flight Lieutenant Bill Craigen and published here for the first time.
(*W. Craigen*)

Centre picture:
Instruments were grouped on a curved panel, showing the Revi reflector gun-sight, with the compass mounted on the right. Note the spare ammunition drums for the MG 15 machine gun on the left behind pilot's seat. (*W. Craigen*)

Soon people were swarming all over the Ju88, some looking for a souvenir. Later, Geoff Whittle (who was left to guard the aeroplane with his mate) decided to get inside for a look around. Suddenly they heard a loud ticking sound. Thinking it was a time bomb, they jumped down and ran for cover, but after a while realised that the ticking was coming from the engines which were still cooling down.

The Ju88A-5, Werke Nr 1624 from IIIKG1, had been on a raid on Liverpool flown by Leutnant Herbert Florian and a crew of three. After bombing Liverpool the radio operator transmitted a message, 'Attack carried out am returning to base'. Almost immediately the starboard engine started to give trouble, and the plane began to judder. Whilst making his bombing run over Liverpool, Florian had taken the Ju88 low over the city and into flak, and it was then, according to crew member Ferdinand Wuhr, that damage to the engine and rudder was done. Within minutes the engine caught fire. Florian knew they could not reach their base and decided to make an emergency landing on one engine. Although it has never been completely proven that this was the reason for the landing at Steeple Morden, it is equally possible that British 'electronic counter measures' (namely Meacon) had been responsible as it was possible to falsify the transmissions of German radio navigation beacons, and that Florian imagined he was over France and not England. But we shall have to

Above:
Interior of Ju88 A-5 (6214) at
Steeple Morden, showing
instrument panel and compass.
(W. Craigen)

wait until the year 2016 as there is a 75 year restriction on German interrogation reports.

The damage to the Ju88's undercarriage and starboard engine was such that it was of little use, so it was dismantled and taken to Royal Aircraft Establishment at Farnborough for investigation of its equipment. Subsequently it was used as spares to keep other Ju88s flying with the RAF's Enemy Aircraft Flight.

On 17 February 1941 the High Commissioner for New Zealand, the Rt Hon W. J. Jordon, was visiting Bassingbourn and was taken to Steeple Morden to be shown over the crashed German Ju88. While there he also took the opportunity of meeting some of his countrymen who were training there at the time.

On the 25th a signal was received from the AOC-in-C Bomber Command which read, 'Please convey my congratulations to the Officer Commanding No 11 OTU and all concerned for the smart bit of work on the night of 15/16 February 1941, when the crew of a Ju88 were taken prisoner at Steeple Morden'.

The Station Commander also commended the following people for their initiative and prompt action which prevented the German crew from destroying their aircraft and papers from which valuable information was obtained: Flight Lieutenant W.J.E. Craigen—Officer in Charge Night Flying;

German Ju88 A-5 (6214) after its crash landing at Steeple Morden, 16.2.41., being inspected by the High Commissioner for New Zealand, the Right Hon W. J. Jordon. (*IWM*)

Sergeant H. E. Bond—Duty Pilot; Aircraftsman 1 H. Boyd, Aircraftsmen 2 M. A. Harran and R. J. Green, the crew of the Armadillo.

With all the flying taking place at Steeple Morden the Germans started to take an even bigger interest in the place. On the night of 26 February at 8.05 pm Steeple Morden was attacked again, probably by NJG2. This German unit, flying Ju88C-2s from its base at Gilze Rijen in Holland, was causing havoc to airfields in East Anglia. Ten bombs were dropped on this occasion and the airfield machine-gunned, the only damage being a small crater on No 3 runway and slight damage to two Wellingtons. One of the ground gunners had a miraculous escape that night when, during the strafing, two bullets passed through his helmet, one bullet above each ear, the impact of which knocked him out. Surely one of the narrowest escapes of the war. . .

After these raids 20 or so airmen would be given large brooms to sweep the runways clear of debris and shrapnel, to prevent punctures in the Wellingtons' tyres.

About this time, with a German invasion still a possibility Fighter Comman drew up plans to move aircraft from the south to alternative aerodromes further north. Steeple Morden was to get Spitfires from 303 Squadron based at Northolt.

'Nickelling'—leaflet dropping over France—continued in

Christmas Menu for II OTU at Bassingbourn, 1941. Not a bad menu when there was rationing on! (*G. Taylor*)

the month of March 1941. The peace was broken on 31 March. As Jim Powling recalls, night flying was in operation, and he and three friends were sitting in the flight hut when they heard the whistling of a bomb which exploded very close to the hut, throwing earth over the roof. As dawn broke they went outside and noticed the fin of a bomb sticking out of the perimeter track, and further holes in the grass. They all walked over to the first hole, one of them walking on and putting his hand down the next hole and shouting out, 'They all must have been duds!' He then proceeded to look down the others. Seconds later the first one exploded showering them with earth, and with that they ran like hell, losing all interest in souvenirs. The following week, Harold Coates recalls he was driving an old Albion van back to the airfield full of singing airmen after their night flying supper. He pulled up to await a green light from the control van for permission to cross the runway, but instead he got a red light, which normally meant an aircraft was landing or taking off. Almost immediately the red light started to flash furiously on

NEXT WEEK

ROYSTON
AND DISTRICT'S
WAR WEAPONS
WEEK

GET READY TO MAKE YOUR MONEY FIGHT

Our War Weapons Week is coming! It will be our special chance to help pay for the huge armaments needed to win this war. Let us be ready—firms and individuals—to lend our savings to the nation.

INVEST ALL YOU CAN IN

3% SAVINGS BONDS
2½% NATIONAL WAR BONDS
3% DEFENCE BONDS
SAVINGS CERTIFICATES
and
POST OFFICE SAVINGS BANK

Double your Group Subscription. Start a new Group in your factory, office or street. Hit back at Hitler. Hit harder than ever in War Weapons Week.

WHERE TO BUY	
SAVINGS BONDS and WAR BONDS	Bank Stockbroker Post Office
DEFENCE BONDS	Post Office Bank Stockbroker
SAVINGS CERTIFICAT	Post Office

MAKE OUR WAR WEAPONS WEEK

Royston & District's War Weapons Week
April 27th to May 3rd.

EVERY BOMB
BOUGHT NEXT WEEK IS A
BOMB
TO BLOW HITLER FROM HIS BED AT BERCHTESGADEN.

THIS SPACE IS DONATED BY
BISHOPS
HOUSE FURNISHERS,
High Street, ROYSTON.

WE
MAKE YOUR VEHICLES
'PULL'
NOW—
NEXT WEEK
"WAR WEAPONS WEEK"

YOUR Savings will help our Armoured Vehicles to
GIVE HITLER
'THE PUSH'

This space is given by—
LOGSDON'S GARAGE,
Melbourn Street,
ROYSTON, Herts.

and off, then all of a sudden, the runway lights were extinguished. Looking through the window screen Harold could see flashes and hear the sound of machine gun fire in the distance, and soon realised that they were about to become the target of a German night fighter that was strafing the airfield. Due to the noise of the old Albion van ticking over and the singing coming from the back of the van, the other occupants were still oblivious as to what was happening. When they realized they had only a few seconds to get out, it was amazing to see how many bodies managed to squeeze through the one and only door so quickly and take cover. The German aircraft vanished as quickly as it arrived into the darkness without hitting them.

During April every town and village held a War Weapon's Week when people helped raise money for the War Effort. The Wing Commander O/C Flying at Bassingbourn, Hugh Constantine (later Air Chief Marshal Sir Hugh Constantine), was asked to organise a low level flypast of Wellingtons over Royston and surrounding villages, piloting one of the Wellingtons himself. It was a great success and encouraged many people to give generously to this worthy cause. Litlington raised £3,204 and Steeple Morden a staggering £6,558.

PRECAUTIONS

The nearest SENIOR WARDEN is:

Mr Robert Pearce
Cheyney Water Farm Tel 236

Ask him for the name and address of your
nearest local Warden and make a note of it here

Frank Savage
Hay Street

Get to know him now and note any
in the names and addresses given h

or the ringing of a handbell. Have your
If RATTLES have been used warning you
until you hear HANDBELLS.

FIRE PRECAUTIONS

Be ready to deal with an incendi
from your attic NOW, and see th
attic or roof space. Provide two b
if possible, a stirrup hand pump with
producing spray for dealing with the bomb
a jet for tackling the resulting fire.
Have a reserve supply of water in buckets or
used water in bath.
If you have no stirrup hand pump, have own buckets

Chapter 5

Village
Home Front

AIR RAID PRECAUTIONS
HANDBOOK No. 2
(2nd Edition)

FIRST AID FOR GAS
CASUALTIES

Chapter 5

Village Home Front

As Steeple Morden and surrounding villages were experiencing more and more air raids, the air raid wardens were being kept very busy as the only way to inform the people of an impending raid was for them to cycle around the villages blowing a whistle, later ringing a bell for the all-clear. At night the blackout regulations were rigorously enforced, and the familiar cry, 'Put that light out', echoed around the villages. The Chief Air Raid Warden's Post was situated close to the airfield at Cheney Water Farm on the Litlington Road, the home of the Chief Warden, Mr R. Pearce.

There were to be six authorised wardens in the village, but by the outbreak of war 13 people had enrolled in the ARP. In the event of an air raid, their duties were to advise people where the shelters were, report the fall of bombs and check on damage, and assist the fire brigade and police. The Cambridgeshire County Council had earlier decided to build surface communal air raid shelters in Steeple Morden and Litlington (where one remains to this day), as it was thought that both villages were vulnerable targets being so close to an airfield. A local builder, Mr Arthur Wright, was given the contract for Steeple Morden, and the shelters were erected in Hay Street, Cheney Street, Ashwell Road, Station Road and the Green, but they were hardly ever used; most people preferred to use an Anderson shelter in their garden or a Morrison shelter in the house.

There was one family who, every time there was an air raid, sat on a bench on the recreation ground, and took their chances there. The only time one of the communal surface air raid shelters in Litlington was well used was when a land mine, having lost its parachute, fell heavily and broke in half, landing in a back garden next to Leache's Garage in the Royston Road, and failing to explode.

It would seem that night the entire population of Litlington

Mr Robert Pearce, chief air-raid warden for Steeple Morden.

Guilden Morden ARP complete with Stirrup Pump, Bell Whistle, and Tin Hat. L/R F. Webb, H. Dellar, B. Warboys, W. Deller, W. G. Deller, F. Raynor. (*John Dellar*)

The only surviving civilian air shelter in Litlington. This one is in the Royston Road. (*Author*)

was evacuated, but many of the occupants of Royston Road decided to squeeze into one shelter, until the mine was safely defused the following morning by a naval officer. The villagers, grateful that the land mine was now safe, made a collection for the brave officer, but he was unable to accept it since regulations forbade him from accepting gifts.

The sequel to this story is that one of the airmen from the airfield billeted in the Royston Road also had a lucky escape that night. On returning from leave in the early hours, having walked from Royston Station to Litlington, he arrived at his billet and was unable to arouse anyone to let him in. Knowing the bedroom windows were never locked, he went round the back, and with the help of a convenient tree climbed in. Very early the next morning he was puzzled to find he was the sole occupant of the house, and was locked in. Due on duty at 7 am, he jumped out of the window and ran across the fields to the airfield, where he was told that the garden next to where he was billeted was where the unexploded land mine was. It was said he never really recovered from the shock!

The villagers of Steeple Morden were very thankful for the generosity of one man, Mr Charles Rigg, who lived at the White House (now a nursing home), when he decided to purchase an air raid siren for the village. (Air raid sirens were normally only sited in large towns.) Once consent was granted by the County Council, it was erected at Savage's Garage in Hay Street, so now the village received plenty of warning of an air raid. Officially there was to be about five minutes' notice of an impending air raid, so long as there was someone at the garage to answer the 'phone and start the siren, recalls John Savage.

The Steeple Morden Air Raid Siren that was sited at Savage's Garage in Hay Street, Steeple Morden. (Now in the Lew Hitch Collection) (*Author*)

Another fear early in the war was a gas attack, and Charlie Potten was appointed the village Gas Identification Officer. Everybody in the village had been issued with a gas mask in 1939, children and babies getting special ones. People were urged to carry them everywhere they went, but all too soon they were forgotten. Near the airfield special boards were placed which would change colour in the event of a mustard gas attack. Fortunately mustard gas was never used, but, unknown at the time, a large quantity was being stored at nearby Bassingbourn airfield.

Despite now having an air raid siren in the village, it was of little use when a lone bomber dropped through the clouds without the siren being sounded, as Frank Huffer recalls. It was the 'Wednesday German' as he got to be known, as on days of very low cloud and especially Wednesdays this German, probably a Ju88 bomber, would dive out of the clouds and circle very low, so low another villager recalls that you could touch it with a clothes prop, you could even see the pilot in the cockpit looking for the airfield to attack, before he would make off very fast, eastwards.

Air Raid Precautions Badge. (*Wills's Cigarettes*)

In nearby Ashwell, one moonlit night, a lone German bomber flew low over the village, no doubt looking for the airfield. On seeing the church spire shining in the moonlight he released a stick of small bombs over the village. Luckily they fell harmlessly on the edge of the village. The following morning one of the bombs which failed to explode was found in a wood shed by Fred Sheldrick. About a week later a train was machine gunned between Ashwell and Baldock. Fortunately nobody was injured.

Steeple Morden only received one really big bomb, a land mine, which landed in the field next to Trap Road. The crater it made, they say, you could put a house in. On another occasion

WILLS'S CIGARETTES

MEDIUM TRAILER FIRE-PUMP

The Mordens NFS Fire Engine and trailer pump and crew. L/R Jack Covington, Sim Star, Jeff Stenton and Lew Hitch.
(L. Hitch)

Card insert above:
A similar type of trailer pump that was used early in the war at Steeple Morden.
(*Wills's Cigarettes*)

flares were dropped with incendiary bombs close to Cheney Water Farm, and numerous fires were started, but fortunately airmen returning in a lorry to the airfield helped the fire watchers and wardens to put the fires out before too much damage was done.

The fire watchers' role was to patrol different parts of the village when there was an alert. One section's duty was to patrol from the pillar box at the Vicarage (now Cheneybury) to Baileys at the Ashwell turning. This was done by F. Oyston, C. Potten, W. Hitch, G. Parrish, J. Jarman, V. South, R. Hitch, L. Hitch, Miss Knight, C. Crow, T. Carter, G. Chubb, B. Unsworth, J. Unsworth, S. Ball, P. M. South and Mrs Grey. Later in the war fire watching was to become compulsory, and everybody in the village was to get involved. As well as having air raid wardens and fire watchers, the village had its own AFS (Auxiliary Fire Service).

The fire engine, a Coventry Climax trailer pump, was towed by an ageing Hillman car painted light grey and was kept in a garage in Cheney Street. Later in the war, after losing their garage facilities, the crews combined with the Guilden Morden AFS and used their fire engine, but this meant having to sleep two nights a week at Town Farm, Guilden Morden, on a 10 pm to 6 am shift.

By 1945 the combined strength of the AFS in the Mordens

was 24, those who joined up being Lew Hitch, Wally Moss, Bill Darts, Ern Rogers, Bill Covington, Will Jarman, Albert Kirbyshire, Bill Charter, Ern Thompson, Bill Millar, Norman Hitch and Frank Huffer from Steeple Morden; and Punch Bonfield, Jack Covington, George Tidy, Jeff Stenton, Sim Starr, Fred Clements, George Merrill, Maurice Rose, Bill Conder, Albert Conder, Arthur Dellar and Rupert Dellar from Guilden Morden.

To assist the local constabulary, eight Special Constables were also appointed, Russel Fordham, Vic Webb, Arthur Wright, Ernie Pepper, Ernie Jarman, John Savage, Reg Hutcherson and Charlie Potten, who was already the Gas Identification Officer. Their main job was to assist the regular police and patrol the village, make sure the blackout regulations were not being broken, check identity cards, and be on look out for 'Fifth Columnists', i.e., traitors. There was a scare in the village that an enemy Fifth Columnist was living in the village as on two occasions, when the airfield was attacked, sheaves of corn were set alight in line with the airfield, using a lighted cigarette in a box of matches, but the culprit was never found.

Charlie Potten also found time to join the Red Cross and was put in charge of First Aid, but said he did not mind as

Steeple Morden and Guilden Morden National Fire Service crews outside their Head-quarters, Town Farm, Guilden Morden. L/R 'Punch' Bonfield, Jack Covington, Lew Hitch, Wally Moss, Bill Darts, Ernie Rogers, George Tidy, Jeff Stenton, Sim Starr, Fred Clements, George Merrill, Maurice Rose, Bill Condor, Albert Condor, Arthur Deller, Rupert Deller, Bill Covington, L. Hitch.

Facing page top:
Red Cross Nurses from Guilden Morden. (*J. Deller*)

Facing page bottom:
Litlington Home Guard. L/R Arthur Covington, Fred Bird, Bill Morris, Arthur Spatchman, Ernie Bonnett, Glem Leach, Arthur Watts, ? Spatchman, Harry Chavett, George King, Arthur Ford, ------ Sgt. George Horsman. (*Arthur Covington*)

Sgt. Harry Wilson and Sgt. Albert Peckett outside the barn used by the Home Guard to store ammunition, which was at the rear of the 'Waggon and Horses'. (*L. Hitch*)

this meant him getting another new uniform. Exercises were carried out in the village with the ARP rescuing people through windows and over stiles, much to the amusement of the local children.

As it was anticipated that there could be many casualties from air attacks, doctors were asked to give First Aid lectures. Two local doctors, Dr John and Dr Sheila Moynihan gave these to all the voluntary services at the school. In Guilden Morden, Morden House was earmarked for the emergency mortuary for the surrounding villages, but thankfully was never used.

In the village the WVS and the Ladies Home Knitting Band were also doing their bit by knitting home comforts for the troops. In one year they completed 97 sea boot stockings, 195 pairs of socks, 24 pairs of mittens, 17 balaclavas, 67 scarves, 44 pairs of gloves and 8 pullovers.

Although food rationing was introduced in 1940 the village was pretty well self sufficient, as many people were already growing their own vegetables. Allotments became very popular, with people being urged to 'Dig For Victory'. The local farmers were also being urged to plough up every available piece of land. Initially butter, sugar and bacon were rationed with 4 oz of butter, 12 oz of sugar and 4 oz of bacon per person per week. Later in the war many other food stuffs were to disappear under the counter, one that hurt the most was tea, which led to tea leaves being used many times. Eggs, although not rationed were termed 'controlled distribution'. One local farmer and a local publican were taken to court for selling eggs to a bus conductor for 4 shillings and 2 pence per score instead of the maximum price of 3 shillings and 4 pence per score. With petrol rationed for the private motorist, it wasn't long before petrol and oil from the airfield found its way into local cars. This stopped after a number of airmen were arrested and court marshalled.

Like all villages, Steeple Morden had its own Home Guard Platoon which, in the beginning, was called the LDV (Local Defence Volunteers) which was also known affectionately as the 'Look, Duck and Vanish' brigade. Renamed the Home Guard after Dunkirk, it was following the broadcast by Anthony Eden on 14 May 1940 that every town and village answered the call and very soon some 250,000 men had joined up. They were given armbands, but guns were initially in very short supply and most villagers had to use their own shotguns or any other weapons they may have had.

Later, uniforms and rifles were issued, and the Home Guard was put on a proper military footing, the village platoon eventually getting a spigot mortar. A handy list of useful German words was also issued, such as: 'Hände hoch'—

Billy Oyston's wedding at
St Peter and St Paul Church,
Steeple Morden, with a Home
Guard, Guard of Honour.
(*Lew Hitch*)

Charlie Potten in his brand new
Red Cross uniform. 1940.
(*Charlie Potten*)

Hands up! and 'Waffen hinliegen'—Thrown Down Your
Arms! Although some people thought of them as a joke, they
still trained with serious intent, as they were aware that in the
event of an invasion they would be called upon to engage and
hamper the enemy. Some of the first to join up in the village
were First World War veterans, together with estate owners,
farmers, bakers and builders. One of the first functions of the
Home Guard was 'stand to' at dusk and watch for landings of
parachutists. This led to many amusing incidents, as one of
the platoon invariably said, 'Halt foe, who goes there?'

One of the observation posts in the village was the top of
the windmill in Ashwell Road, which, by all accounts was fine
in the summer, but very bleak in winter time.

Another task was to check that motor vehicles were
immobilised at night, but this nearly caused the death of two
of the village platoon. After leaving the 'Waggon and Horses',
Aubrey Wright and Jack Newell came across a car parked in
a driveway in Hay Street. On opening the door Aubrey tried
the starter button, causing the car to start, so deciding the
car was not properly immobilised he decided to let the tyres
down. All of a sudden an upstairs window burst open and an
RAF officer who was billeted there leant out waving a pistol,
shouting, 'Halt, or I'll shoot'. With that, Aubrey and Jack
took to their heels as bullets ricocheted off the road and
rooftops.

Forty-five people joined the Home Guard from the village,
Tom Jarman being appointed 1st Lieutenant, George Smyth
2nd Lieutenant, Albert Peckett, Harry Wilson, Mick Moss
and Bill Oyston Sergeants while Stan Izzard and Les Pearce

were Corporals. The Privates were Jack, Reg, Norman, Will and Tom Jarman, Jack Newell, Harry Smith, Bill and Harold Peckett, Charlie Crow, Frank Westrope, Syd and Bill Moule, Bill Moss, Alec Jennings, Vic South, Aubrey Wright, George Barnes, John Brockett, Theo Saunderson, John and Ralph Mcavoy, Jim Parker, Bob Unsworth, Sid Ball, Graham Parrish, George Brown, Ernie Willmott, Jim Turnham, Bill Brown, Bill Attridge, Len Moss, Albert 'Sonny' Webb, Bill Newland, Ron Ward, George Ebdon and George Chubb.

The local school was used as the headquarters for the Home Guard, meetings being held in the evenings, with drill on Sunday mornings on the Recreation Ground, and occasional gas training at Bassingbourn airfield. Stan Izzard recalls everyone hated gas training because if you didn't have your gas mask adjusted right, your eyes streamed, and you nearly choked to death.

Rifle practice was carried out at the chalk pit, and it was during training here that the whole platoon nearly got wiped out. Whilst having instruction with a newly issued Sten Gun, Ernie Willmott got it stuck on continuous fire, and then turned round for help, sending the whole platoon diving for cover. Luckily someone threw himself at Ernie, knocking him to the ground and saving the platoon. . .

Steeple Morden Home Guard Platoon. Circa 1940. (*A. Wright*)

Exercises were also carried out with platoons from surrounding villages, and a mock invasion of the village was carried out. This sometimes proved to be a humorous affair as the opposing platoon were said to be cheating by invading across the fields and not up the High Street as expected. The Station Commander at the airfield issued a challenge to the village platoon, to test out his defences. The following night, under the cover of darkness, the Steeple Morden platoon borrowed some ladders from a local decorator, laid them across the river at Lower Gatley Farm and managed to climb inside a Wellington bomber. The Station Commander was furious that, as he put it, 'a band of amateurs had got in' and he ordered a shake up of the airfield's defences.

As so much land was requisitioned for the airfield, some of the local farmers asked for permission to farm inside the perimeter. This was granted but one local farmer, Frank Huffer, recalls this could be quite dangerous with aircraft taking off and landing. He also managed to cut the underground telephone wire with his plough a few times. Another

The Litlington and Abington Pigotts Home Guard Platoon outside St Catherine's Church, Litlington.
(*Evelyn Huffer*)

incident for which the local farmers got the blame, was when some horses strayed onto the aerodrome at night. With the airmen chasing them up and down the runways in total darkness, one airman recalls it was like a western 'Rodeo'. It was not until daylight that they could be sure that all the horses had been rounded up, and flying could start again.

Mr Frank Huffer's Barrier Pass for Steeple Morden Airfield issued in January 1942. This pass allowed him to farm inside the perimeter fence. (*Mr Frank Huffer*)

No. 3

Chapter 6

The Training Continues

Chapter 6

The Training Continues

Despite the bombing of the airfield and the bad weather, 11 OTU managed to log, on 31 March, 1429 hours daytime flying and 417 hours night flying and had an output of 15 pilots, five observers and two wireless operator/air gunners.

On the night of 10 April at 10.16 pm the Germans from NJG2 found Steeple Morden again. Ten high explosive bombs (only one of which exploded) caused a small crater in the runway and injured one airman. At approximately 12.40 am they returned, this time dropping eight HE bombs and a number of incendiaries which temporarily stopped night flying.

To help prevent these attacks, 'Q' sites were set up. These were dummy or decoy airfields built to look like authentic ones in the hope that the enemy would bomb them instead of the real ones. Bassingbourn and Steeple Morden's 'Q' site was at Manor Farm, Barley (a T-type No 37), but it drew off few attacks. Only recently, during a clear-out of a barn at Manor Farm, some of the old landing lights were found together with fragments of German bomb casings. A second site was at Caxton Gibbet which was also an Elementary Flying Training School. This site was more successful, as it had had some old 'Wimpys' and a Chance light. Ground crews were detached there at night but it was not a popular place as they had to sleep in a derelict farmhouse on the edge of the airfield (which by all accounts was haunted), so after many sleepless nights, of strange noises, and bolted doors opening, most of the ground crews preferred to sleep in tents. Steeple Morden also tried putting out extra flare paths as decoys. When the air raid warning was sounded, this was supposed to divert attacks from Bassingbourn, but it was not very successful.

On 10 April, just as a Wellington 1s(*L4253*) was doing a last circuit of the airfield, it was shot down by an unidentified enemy aircraft, crashed near Ashwell Station and was burnt out. Luckily both pilot and pupil escaped without injury.

Eight days later at 2.15 am a Wellington Mk1—*L4302*—on circuit training stalled whilst undershooting at low altitude at Steeple Morden and crashed at Abington Pigotts, killing both members of the crew, Pilot Officer H. H. Boiler and Sergeant F. Fulford. This brought the total to 29 crew members missing or killed whilst training since 1940 with 11 OTU.

With the Germans now flying virtually unopposed over the area, they shot down another Wellington (*N2912*) on the 24th over Bassingbourn with the aircraft crashing onto another Wellington (*R1404*) at its dispersal, injuring the pilot and killing the other two members of the crew.

On Monday, 29 April 1941, the dockyards at Plymouth and Devonport were the main German targets, over 124 aircraft of Luftflotte 2 and 3 being responsible. At approximately 11.57 pm a lone bomber attacked Steeple Morden, dropping one HE 50kg bomb which, fortunately, failed to explode. When it was defused the following day it was found to be of an unusual type, containing 20lb of TNT plus incendary units. The following day 11 OTU lost another Wellington (*T2905*) when it flew into a balloon cable and crashed at St Andrews Park, Bristol, killing the crew of six. Thirteen days later the airfield was attacked again. This time 12 HE bombs were dropped, one failing to explode, plus three baskets of incendiaries. Only one airman was injured by bomb splinters.

1/NJG2 claimed another victim on 7 May when Wellington *N3227* was coming in to land. At 900ft a Ju88 attacked; the rear gunner, Sergeant Stuart, returned the fire but it was too late as the port wing tank was on fire. Unable to make the airfield, Flying Officer Warner force landed at Wendy village. Both Warner and his pupil Pilot Officer McNally were thrown out through the escape hatch. Sergeant Stuart was also thrown clear, all three escaping with cuts and bruises.

On 29 May at 1.20 am a mechanic, Aircraftsman Worthington, who had just returned from leave after getting married, accidentally walked into a propeller of a Wellington as the chocks were being pulled away and was instantly killed. The following night Flying Officer Lorne Curry, waiting at the end of the runway to take off, jumped down from his aircraft to warn an aircraft that it was heading for a sheer drop at the end of the runway. Unfortunately, he ran straight into an approaching aircraft's propeller. Two identical deaths on two consecutive nights, but unfortunately many aircrew and groundcrew were to meet with this terrible death when working on blacked out airfields at night.

It was not until 5 June 1941 that the aerodrome was raided again, bombs cratering No 2 runway and stopping the night flying. Then on 9 June, a cross-country flying exercise ended in disaster. At 3.10 pm Wellington *R1728* took off from

At dusk Wellington crews board for another flight.

(*Crown copyright*)

Steeple Morden with a crew of seven Flying Officers, W. L. Foster (captain), Pilot Officer C.W.S. Bristov (2nd pilot), Sergeant R. P. Burt (observer), Sergeant L. Parry (1st wireless operator), Sergeant E. G. Buckingham (2nd wireless operator), and Sergeant G.N.W. Hare (airgunner). Their route took them over the North Sea where all contact was lost; it was later presumed that they had crashed into the sea. It was not until nearly three weeks later that an RAF launch found a dinghy off the Humber at Bridlington, which contained the bodies of Sergeants Hare and Burt.

The middle of June was to see yet another Wellington (*R1292*) crash west of Wendy village. 'Nickel' dropping over France still carried on throughout June and a total of 1,892 hours of day flying and 1,158 hours of night flying was achieved from Bassingbourn and Steeple Morden. But on 8 July Wellington *L4355*, attempting to land at Steeple Morden, crashed at Litlington, killing the crew of three; then on the 18th the crew of Wellington 1C *X3169* had a lucky escape: as they attempted to land they were machine-gunned by a enemy Ju88, but the aircraft managed to land safely, the crew uninjured.

On 22 July the crew of Wellington *R1334* were not so lucky. Piloted by Sergeant Pilot F. S. Housten and flying through light rain at 1.30 am, they were circling in an anti-clockwise direction waiting for their turn to land at Steeple

Sergeant Reg Hibbert who was the front gunner of the Welling-ton Ic, *R1334*, that collided with the Ju88 over Ashwell church, 22 July 1941. (*G. F. Stanford*)

Morden after a cross-country training flight. Three pilots, four wireless operators and an observer were on board. When at 600 feet over Ashwell Church they collided with Ju88C-4 Werke Nr 0842, *R4+BL*, flown by Leutnant Volker and his two crewmen, Feldwebel (Flight Sergeant) Andreas Wurski and Unteroffizer (Sergeant) Herbert Indentbirken. The Ju88 was apparently circling in a clockwise direction. Both aircraft exploded in a ball of flame which was seen for miles around, and watched in horror by the other Wellington crews who were waiting to land. All the eight crew were killed in the Wellington and the three Germans in the Ju88. Blazing fuel and the main wreckage fell in the fields and gardens on the edge of Ashwell village, the tail of the German Ju88 landing in the High Street. The following day at the crash site an officer from the RAF's Air Intelligence Section AI1(g), found that the armament had been increased. Three MG17s and a 20mm cannon were in the nose, and in a lower gondola another 20mm cannon. A German satchel was found, containing recognition flares used by the RAF together with a German map case, with maps showing all the airfields in the area, and a route from the coast which avoided all our known Ack-Ack sites. Also found was a clothing tag with the name 'Oberfahrnrich H. Volker', and it was soon realised that this was Leutnant Heinze Volker, the ace of 3/NJG2 with seven claims to his credit—he had nearly got his eighth. Only quite recently the field on the edge of Ashwell where his aircraft fell was the scene of an archaeological dig. Various parts were found from the Ju88, and these have been donated to the Ashwell Museum by Mr Eric Gurney on whose land they fell.

Leutenant Heinze Volker (left) and Leutenant Johannes Fuerbaum in the cockpit of a Ju88. Just prior to Volker's death when his Ju88 collided with a Wellington over Ashwell on 22.7.41.
(*S. W. Parry*)

Before the end of the month two more Wellingtons, *N2747* and *R1148*, were to crash, the first at Whaddon village and the second at Spalding, Lincs, whilst on training flights, killing six and injuring three. On 13 August the Ju88s from Gilze-Rijen left Steeple Morden alone and bombed Bassingbourn with devastating results, four high explosive bombs and incendiaries being dropped and the airfield machine-gunned. One wing of the 'H' barrack blocks collapsed and there were 22 casualties, ten of which were fatal. One airman, Jack Redfern, had a lucky escape that night; due to promotion to Corporal he was moved out of the block which was bombed the day before, and thinks his promotion was a gift of life.

Six days later another Wellington, *N3005,* was shot down by a Ju88 from 1/NJG2 flown by Feldwebel Kosler, the aircraft crashing north-east of Barrington killing three of the crew and injuring one. This was the seventh Wellington lost to 1/NJG2. Before the month was out, Bassingbourn was raided yet again, nine bombs being dropped on the taxiway, stopping all flying due to unexploded bombs.

By the end of August 1/NJG2 had made 257 sorties on twenty-six nights, with no less than ninety-four attacks on airfields in the south-east. But this level of operations could not be substained as their losses were starting to mount.

An airfield in the village became a magnet for the local children who sat for hours watching the Wellington bombers doing their circuits and bumps, but some could not resist a closer look. Don Hitch and his brother Lew, Doug Hart, Frank Oyston and Tony Jarman crawled under the barbed

Wellington IC *R1334* with 'D' Flight ground crew at Steeple Morden. Just prior to its collision with a Ju88 over Ashwell on 22.7.41. (*G. Tyack*)

The crash as reported in the Royston Crow
(*County Records Office Hertford*)

EARLY MORNING AIR CRASH

R.A.F. Plane and Junker Collide Near Village

A German bomber and a British plane collided over a village in the Home Counties in the early hours of Tuesday morning. They fell in fields a mile apart, and caught fire.

The bodies of the British and two German airmen were recovered, and it was at first thought that another German might have escaped by parachute, but it was later decided that he had been caught in the plane and burned.

An unexploded bomb was found lying near the German plane, and Junkers.

There were no civilian casualties, and no damage was caused.

wire at Gatley End. Don and Tony climbed inside one of the Wellingtons and were having great fun playing with the controls. Then, on coming down the ladder, they noticed that the ground crew had left some nuts and bolts from the engine covers and so they decided to keep a few as souvenirs. Minutes later they were spotted by the RAF guards who were on patrol on bicycles. The four of them ran like mad, throwing their souvenirs into the river as the guards shouted and waved their rifles at them. The incident scared them so much they never tried it again, as they thought they might have been mistaken for saboteurs.

The weather in August was good and the training continued at Bassingbourn and Steeple Morden with an output of 27 Wellington crews and an establishment of 54 Wellingtons, and 18 Avro Ansons and 2 Lysanders. 'Nickel' dropping over France carried on from the 2nd to the 17th; as well as carrying leaflets, some aircraft carried a small amount of bombs. Occasionally leaflets were wrapped around a few wine bottles, and thrown out for good measure, making a frightening whistling noise as they fell.

With all this training the airmen and WAAFs looked forward to their off-duty hours, many of them cycling on their newly issued Hercules cycles to Royston, or as far afield as Letchworth to go to the cinema. Popular films showing at the time were 'Sailors Three' starring Tommy Trinder and Claude Hulbert and 'My Little Chickadee' starring Mae West and W. C. Fields. One of the other things to do was to visit one of the many pubs in the area. In Steeple there were plenty to choose from; there was 'The Fox', 'Carriers', 'The

Still wearing the code of 215 this Wellington No 2912 was shot down over Basssingbourn by a Ju88 and crashed onto R1404 at its dispersal. (M.J.F. Bowyer)

Waggon and Horses', 'The Green Man', 'The Bell', and the 'Plough'. And at the other end of the airfield at Litlington was the 'Crown', 'The Seven Stars', 'The Beehive' and the 'Royal Oak' which had a handy air raid shelter next door to it, but many preferred to go to the Chapel School Rooms which opened in the evenings as a canteen, run by the local WVS with hot buttered toast and poached eggs being the firm favourites. On Sundays the men were encouraged to stay for the communal singing. Two of the favourite places in Royston were the 'Railway Tavern' and the 'Green Plunge' restaurant and swimming pool. On one occasion a Wellington which had just taken off from Bassingbourn decided to 'shoot up' the swimming pool, flying so low, it is said, that it ruffled the water, and just missed some trees near the pool. Dancing was also very popular but this meant going to Cambridge or London by train. Many lasting friendships were made with local girls and with the WAAFs billeted in Litlington, a few eventually getting married. One instructor recalls his wonderful honeymoon he spent in a cottage in Abington Pigotts, which was opposite the pub, 'The Darby and Joan' now called the 'Pig and Abbott', and remembers he was either in bed, or in the pub – absolute bliss!

September of 1941 was another good month with 61 pilots, 31 observers, 64 wireless/air gunners and 25 air gunners completing their training, flying some 2,314 hours.

On 4 September, according to the operations log at Steeple Morden, the airfield was bombed by a Blenheim. This British bomber apparently dropped two bombs on the edge of the airfield at 1.32 pm, causing no damage except livening up a quiet lunchtime. There was a rumour in the village at the time that the Blenheim was, in fact, an aircraft that had crash-landed in France, and that it was being flown by a German crew who had been at the university in Cambridge, but this was never proved.

September and October were again good months for weather and a considerable amount of training was done, but no 'Nickelling' operations were carried out. December saw the temporary transfer of 'A' flight from Bassingbourn to Steeple Morden and 'C' and 'E' to Tempsford due to the construction of runways at Bassingbourn. One other important event which happened in December was the decision by the German High Command to suspend operations over Britain of 1/NJG2, and that they were to move immediately to Sicily for operations in the Mediterranean theatre. The news of the move was welcomed by the RAF as they had lost 21 Wellingtons to the Junkers Ju88 intruders from Gilze-Rijen in as many months. After losing so many aircraft, 11 OTU Wellingtons were slowly being replaced by Wellington 1cs.

Sergeant Thompson and his W.A.A.F. wife. They met whilst both were serving at Steeple Morden. After their marriage she was immediately posted away. (G. F. Stanford)

'The Plough' Steeple Morden. (M. Huffer)

Early in 1942 another type of aircraft landed at Steeple Morden, a Hampden (*P5235*) from Swinderby in Yorkshire, which was forced to land due to running low on fuel after a mine-laying operation.

So into 1942 the careful training of aircrew continued, but on 10 January Wellington *X9796* made such a heavy landing that the undercarriage collapsed, and on the 26th two Wellingtons collided whilst taxying.

The early part of January 1942 started off very cold and wet, and night flying was continually being cancelled due to the bad weather. Jack Redfern recalls he was called into the watch office by the Duty Night Flying Officer to be told that flying was scrubbed yet again. But a message had just been received that a Short Stirling (*N6102*) from Mildenhall, returning from an operational mission, was in the circuit and was very short of fuel. Due to the prevailing wind the pilot was told to use No 1 runway, which was the longest at Steeple Morden but barely long enough for the four-engined Stirling to land.

The villagers of Litlington must have wondered what all the noise was as the Stirling made two practice approaches over the village. The pilot then called Flying Control and said that next time he was going to put it down as he was almost out of fuel. The crash tender and ambulance, now alerted, waited at the end of the runway as the Stirling swept in with its landing lights blazing in the gloom, barely missing the top of Litlington church. The pilot managed to touch down well up the runway, giving himself the full length to land, and after running out of runway the pilot just managed to stop the Stirling on the grass at the far end of the airfield.

The crash tender and ambulance were soon at the scene, but fortunately were not required. The crew were all very relieved after such a 'dicey' landing and were full of praise for their skipper for managing to land such a big bomber on such a short runway. After refuelling the following day, the Stirling was flown back to Mildenhall.

The following night two Whitleys landed. *L9314* from 51 Squadron came first due to bad weather, and then at 2.30 am *L9232* from 138 Squadron landed short of fuel after being on a secret mission. Heavy snow fell the following day, resulting in Operation 'Snow Plan' being put into use, which meant a lot of hard work to keep the runways clear.

On 10 February, 11 OTU suffered a staggering blow when Wellington *X9905* crashed on a cross country exercise at Harrow Green, Leytonstone, near London, killing the crew of six. Seven days later Wellington *T2717* crashed soon after take off from Steeple Morden, killing the crew of four. But training continued with a new exercise, known as 'Bullseye'. These

Sergeant and Mrs A. Lewis on their wedding day. In 1941 they came to live in Litlington, while Allen, a New Zealander, did his training with 11 OTU. Later in the war Sergeant Lewis was to lose a part of his hand when an incendiary bomb dropped from another Wellington and hit his rear gun turret. (*Sheila Allen*)

Sergeant Eric Shipley and Pilot Officer Frank Crook, 11 OTU. Both were killed when their Wellington crashed at Spalding, Lincs. (*G. F. Stanford*)

were simulated bombing attacks, in which anti-aircraft gun defences and searchlights were used, occasionally with London bridges as the photographic pin-point 'target'. These exercises were to become very important in operational training.

March saw another flying accident, when on the 10th, Wellington *L4382* swung on landing to avoid another aircraft and crashed, fortunately with no casualties. Again, on the 12th, another Wellington, *L4351*, made a very heavy landing and crashed. Further crashes were Wellington *X9796* on the 15th and *R1081* on the 23rd. With all these crashes one piece of equipment that every crew member made sure he had with him was his parachute. You can imagine one crew member's

The only artwork allowed was a chalked-on girl's name—Phyllis!
(*Lionel Hughes*)

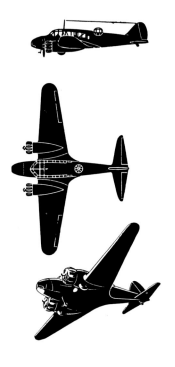

horror when he ripped his parachute, which meant pulling the rip cord so it could be re-packed, and found that all it contained was a blanket.

To flush out who could be responsible all the parachute packers were taken up in an aeroplane and told they were going to make a parachute jump. One of them, realising he might be wearing a chute with only a blanket inside, broke down and admitted that he was the culprit. At a later court of inquiry it was found out that the parachute silk was being sold on the black market. Luckily it didn't end in tragedy. Later in the month a Spitfire (YQ-F) of 616 Squadron (Wittering) was abandoned after colliding with another aircraft and crashed near Bassingbourn, the pilot parachuting to safety.

April brought another four-engined aircraft, a Halifax, serial number *R1002*, from 138 Squadron down onto Steeple Morden's runway after it had been on a clandestine mission from its base at Tempsford. Due to the secrecy of the mission it was requested that the Czech pilot should not be interrogated until he returned to Tempsford. Wellington *L9014* also found its way down onto Steeple Morden's runway on 10 April. The crew were all very relieved at getting back safely from a training flight when, all of a sudden, they heard a terrible noise. It was then that the pilot, Sergeant Croall, realised that he had not lowered the undercarriage. Luckily, all the crew escaped without injury.

On 11 April an Avro Anson, *R9704*, flown by Flight Sergeant Taylor, crashed on take off, the crew escaping without injury. On the 25th the crew of Wellington *R1661* from Steeple Morden were not so fortunate. Whilst coming in to land at Waddington airfield in Lincolnshire, they undershot and crashed, killing three and seriously injuring the others.

During March and April, 'Bullseye' exercises continued together with bombing practice at various ranges on the east coast. Some of these were carried out at night, but the daytime ones, according to the Operations Record book, were the more accurate. Using 11½lb practice bombs the daytime average error was 162 yards and at night it was 179 yards, hardly surprising considering the basic navigation and bomb aiming equipment available at the time. In April a total of 1,921 practice bombs and flares were dropped.

Occasionally a local bombing range was used this was at Croydon Wilds, between Gransden and Longstowe. On one occasion a Wellington was loaded with live bombs instead of practice bombs, and by all accounts frightened the poor range officer to death. Nearby Duxford, a fighter base, also had a narrow escape when a Wellington, from Steeple Morden, making its approach to the Croydon Wilds Range, opened its bomb bay doors and, to the crew's horror, the practice bombs fell out onto the airfield, fortunately without causing any injuries or damage. It was later discovered that this was due to an electrical fault in the bomb release mechanism. After this incident the Commanding Officer at Duxford understandably couldn't find any kind words for trainee bomber crews! But all too soon all this bombing training was to be put to good use.

Leading Aircraftsman Lionel Hughes sitting on a Wellington named 'Floss' at Steeple Morden. Note: the front machine guns have been removed.

(*Lionel Hughes*)

Chapter 7

The Thousand Plan

Banquet Exercise

Previous page:
Wellington Is of the type used
by II O.T.V.
(*M.O.D.*)

Chapter 7

The
Thousand Plan
Banquet Exercise

It was the appointment of Arthur Harris as Commander-in-Chief, RAF Bomber Command, and his controversial ideas that were to change the air war. In early May of 1942 he put a plan to the Prime Minister, Winston Churchill, for a 1,000 Bomber Raid on a German city, with a view to wiping it out in one night. By 26 May it was decided that Hamburg was to be attacked with Cologne as the alternative target. The mission was to be mounted in the last week of May which was a full moon period. As the news of the operation reached Bassingbourn, telegrams were dispatched to all the air crews on leave to return immediately, and all further leave cancelled. To get 1,000 Bombers meant that anything that could fly had to go. This operation was also to involve Operational Training Units and 11 OTU was to supply 25 Wellingtons, 12 from Bassingbourn and 13 from Steeple Morden. On the airfield everybody helped to get the aircraft ready, no matter what their trades were, sometimes working all night, as every aircraft had to be one hundred percent airworthy. By the 30th the weather was to be the deciding factor as to which target was to be attacked, as the operation had already been postponed on three successive days. At 12.30 pm Harris took the decision that Cologne was to be the target. In all 1,046 aircraft took off on 31 May, but rumours of a big raid had been going round the village for days. By early evening the Wellingtons were all lined up and ready to go. Most of the aircraft were loaded with huge canisters of incendiaries and two 500 lb G P bombs. The 13 from Steeple Morden started taking off at 10.28 pm. It should be noted that on these first raids it was mainly the instructors who piloted or navigated the aircraft, often the rest of the crew were made up of trainees facing battle for the first time.

One man who took part in the raid was Pilot Officer Stan Conway. He was a navigator in Wellington *Z8808 (KJ-E)*

Leading Aircraftsman Lionel Hughes and mate astride a Pegasus engine at Steeple Morden.

(Lionel Hughes)

Flight Lieutenant Fletcher at the controls of Wellington *Z8808* which took part in the first 1,000 Bomber raid. Later in the war he was killed on operations. (S. Conway)

Warrant Officer Fredrick James Stanley who was killed on the raid on Essen on 2.6.42., whilst flying Wellington *DV767* from Steeple Morden. (J. Brocket)

from 'X' squadron. His pilot that night was Flight Lieutenant Fletcher, Flight Sergeant Ward was the wireless operator, Sergeant Groves was front air gunner and Flight Lieutenant Craig was rear air gunner. They took off at 10.40 pm, the flight he recalls was uneventful. They formed up to join the Bomber stream on the coast between Southwold and Orfordness then flew across the North Sea, where some cloud and icing were experienced. After crossing the Dutch coast the cloud cleared and Cologne was clearly visible.

Moderate to heavy flak was encountered over the target, but they suffered no casualties, and landed back at Steeple Morden at 3.53 am. On the airfield 'B' flight mechanics were counting the aircraft in until there were only two aircraft missing. As dawn was starting to break, one of the ground crew shouted 'listen' and the unmistakable sound of a Wellington was heard in the distance. Minutes later it touched down and was surrounded by the groundcrew, vans, staff cars, ambulance and the fire tender, the crew being rushed off for interrogation. Later the pilot explained that the reason for being late was that after dropping their bombs they stooged around the city looking at the devastation and fires below, as it seemed as if the whole city was alight. Eight hundred and ninety eight crews claimed to have bombed Cologne. Twenty-two from 11 OTU, one Wellington *R1252 (OP-P)* returning to Bassingbourn early due to a IFF detonator exploding in the wireless operator's face. Only one Wellington from 11 OTU was lost on the raid, Steeple Morden Wellington *R1065 (KJ-Z)*; another crash-landed at Fressingfield after losing a propeller over the target, and *X9614 (TX-J)* force-landed at Oakington after flak damaged one engine, and injured Sergeant Saunders, the front air gunner. The raid was a success in terms of damage to Cologne, but left some four hundred and sixty nine people dead, and five thousand and twenty seven injured, but 40 aircraft failed to return.

With the moon full for a few more nights, Harris decided to bomb Essen on 1 June 1942 and 11 OTU was to send 20 Wellingtons, nine from Bassingbourn, and eleven from Steeple Morden. Stan Conway was again to navigate with the same crew that had been to Cologne the previous night. This time the raid was not so successful due to cloud and haze, but out of some 956 bombers that took off, 767 claimed to have bombed the target. One Wellington from Steeple Morden *DV767 (UP-J)* failed to return, all contact being lost with this aircraft during the mission, with the loss of Warrant Officer Stanley (pilot), Warrant Officer Railton (navigator), Flight Sergeant Kennedy (wireless operator), Sergeant James (front air gunner) and Sergeant Spenceley (rear air gunner). The pilot, Warrant Officer Stanley, had a premonition before the

Extract from Stan Conway's logbook, who was the navigator on Wellington Z8808 which took part in the first 1000 Bomber raid on Cologne, and later Essen, from Steeple Morden. (S. Conway)

Date	Hour	Aircraft Type and No.	Pilot	Duty	Remarks	Day	Night
					Time carried forward:	698:05	215:00
30-5-42	22:30	Z8808	F/Lt Fletcher	Nav	Raid on Cologne		5:25
31-5-42	15.00	Z8808	—"—	—"—	N.F.T.	:20	
1-6-42	11.00	—"—	—"—	—"—	N.F.T.	:15	
1-6-42	23:15	—"—	—"—	—"—	Raid on Essen		4:35
17-6-42	1200	Anson	—"—	—"—	Base – Harwell	:30	
	1400	—"—	—"—	—"—	Harwell – Hampstead Norris	:15	
	1630	—"—	—"—	—"—	Hampstead Norris – Base	:30	

Officer Commanding, Training Wing, R.A.F. BASSINGBOURN, HERTS.

Total Time 699.55

Appendix A.33- A.39.   R.A.F. Form 541.

OPERATIONS RECORD BOOK.

DETAIL OF WORK CARRIED OUT.

From 2228 hrs 30./.5./42 to 0505 hrs 31./.5./42. By No. 11 O.T.U.   No. of pages used for day 4

Place	Date	Time	Summary of Events	References to Appendices
BASSINGBOURN (STEEPLE MORDEN)	30-31.5.42	2228-0420	BANQUET EXERCISE ("THOUSAND PLAN") Attack on COLOGNE.	A.33 to A.57.
			25 Wellingtons, comprising 12 aircraft "X" Squadron BASSINGBOURN and 13 aircraft	B.48
			"Y" Squadron STEEPLE MORDEN took off for attack on COLOGNE. 22 aircraft	D.126
			successfully bombed target causing extensive fires, 1 aircraft bombed DUISBURG	
			DOCKS, 1 aircraft returned to base, 1 aircraft failed to return, 1 aircraft	D.123, D.124
			crash landed FRESSINGFIELD (M7295) 1 aircraft force landed OAKINGTON 1 aircraft	D.125, D.128
			damaged by FLAK.	D.127, D.129
			Bombing results very satisfactory.	
			Weather: Target area - Fine, cloud NIL. Visibility good	
BASSINGBOURN	29.5	0001	STATION DUTIES. S/LDR. W. H. SHAW assumed duties of P.M.C. Officers Mess.	
			F/LT. A.H.N. SNOW assumed duties of Financial and Bar Secretary, Officers Mess.	
BASSINGBOURN	31.5.	2359	NIGHT FLYING SUPPERS. - all personnel, officers, N.C.Os, and airmen to be	
			served in future in the airmens mess.	
	29.5.	0001	Station Duties - P/O W.G.H. GUISELEY assumed duties of Administrative	
			Secretary Officers Mess.	
			SUMMARY FOR THE MONTH OF MAY.	
			INTAKE AND OUTPUT OF PERSONNEL.	

	Pilots	Observers	W/Op Ags.	Ags.	TOTAL.	
INTAKE (Personnel)	13	54	31	26	= 124	D.130
OUTPUT (Personnel	5	3	4	3	= 15	D.131
(Crews	18				= 18 crews	

FLYING TIMES	Hours	Minutes	
DAY	1336	50	
NIGHT	726	05	D.132
TOTAL	2062	55	

Appendix A.33- A.39.   R.A.F. FORM 541.

OPERATIONS RECORD BOOK.

DETAIL OF WORK CARRIED OUT.

From 2228 hrs 30./.5./42 to 0505 hrs 31./.5./42. By No. 11 O.T.U.   No. of pages used for day 4

Aircraft Type and No.	Crew.	Duty.	Time Up.	Time Down.	Remarks.	References.
Wellingtons		Attack on COLOGNE	30-31/5/42.		Aircraft Engaged = 25. Object - Destruction of COLOGNE.	A.33 to A.57
Z.8808 (KJ-E)	F/Lt.Fletcher (Pilot) P/O. Conway (Nav) F/Sgt.Ward (W/Op.) Sgt. Groves (F.AG). F/Lt.Craig (R.AG). ("X" Squadron).	"	2240	0353	Call Sign - 5QXE. Target attacked 2 x 500 GP (N & T inst). 240 x 4 Incend. Bombs dropped 0107-0110 hrs. Ht. 12,000'. Photos - Nil. Results - Bursts observed left bank of RHINE close to aiming point. Moderate to heavy flak deteriorating. No casualties. Weather - Fine. Cloud Nil. Vis. very good.	A.33
Z.8828 (TX-G)	P/O. Wakeford (Pilot) F/O. Anderson (Nav) P/O. Phear (W/Op.) Sgt. Florence (F.AG). F/Sgt. Da Costa (R.AG). ("X" Squadron).	"	2249	0414	Call Sign - XA3G. Target attacked 2 x 500 G.P. (N & T inst). 180 x 4 Incend. Bombs dropped 0054-0122 hrs. Ht. 11,000'. Photos - Nil. Results - bomb bursts observed on target - extensive fires. Flak encountered. No casualties. 2 compartments of 1 S.B.C. incend. failed to release. Weather - Fine. 3/10 Cld. (low) Vis. good.	A.34

mission that he would not return, and asked his wife, who was pregnant at the time with expected twins, to name them Susan and Robert, which she did.

Now having been on raids for two successive nights, the crews were hoping for a stand-down, and at 10.45 am on 2 June 1942 a message was sent from No 91 group that 11 OTU could revert to training. A wave of relief went through the camp. But on the very next day a now familiar accident occurred when Wellington Z8970 landed with its undercarriage retracted, luckily with no casualties.

On the 4th a garden party was thrown at Kneesworth Hall for all the crews and groundstaff who had participated in the Cologne and Essen raids, to thank them for a job well done, and all at the Bassingbourn Station Commander's expense.

Now that operations were off and training could start again, the aircrews at Bassingbourn and Steeple Morden could relax, and, with the arrival in Litlington of 38 more WAAFs in their new billet, things were looking up.

On 10 June six Wellingtons from Steeple Morden demonstrated 'Smoke and Parachute Dropping' with Fighter Command and the C-in-C thought the demonstration was very effective. 'Bullseye' exercises carried on during June, but were marred on the 21st when Wellington R1336 burst a main wheel on take off, crashed and caught fire. Luckily all the crew escaped without injury.

Harris was of the opinion that the large-scale raids should continue during nights of a full moon, so, on 25 June, 11 OTU contributed 25 Wellingtons, 12 from Bassingbourn and 13 from Steeple Morden, to the force of 1,006 aircraft. The target Bremen was coded 'Millenium Two'. Again the target was covered in cloud, but 18 aircraft of 11 OTU attacked the target; two aircraft returned early and one crash-landed at Lower Agney, Kent, all the crew escaping uninjured. Although the raid was a success it nowhere approached that of Cologne. 11 OTU lost three aircraft, all from Steeple Morden: Wellington S3213 (KJ-L), Flight Sergeant Holden (pilot), Sergeant Urquart (navigator), Sergeant Matthewson (wireless operator), Sergeant Mitchell (rear air gunner) and Sergeant Falk (front air gunner); Wellington DV778 (KJ-A), Sergeant Cubitt (pilot), Sergeant Parrish (navigator), Sergeant Wilton (wireless operator), Sergeant Flower (rear air gunner) and Sergeant Mutton (front air gunner); and Wellington R1078 (TX-Q), Pilot Officer King (pilot), Sergeant Main (navigator), Sergeant Barker (wireless operator), Sergeant Reeves (rear air gunner) and Sergeant Holland (front air gunner). All contact was lost with these aircraft during the raid.

One Wellington lucky to make it back that night from Bremen, was Wellington DV 889 (KJ-V) flown by Sergeant Quirk

Facing page:
Extracts from 11 OTU's Operations Record Book showing their part in the First Thousand Bomber Raid on Cologne, 30.5.42. (Crown Copyright by kind permission of Her Majesty's Stationery Office PRO Air 29/642)

and his mainly trainee New Zealand crew. One of the crew, the rear gunner, was Sergeant White, whose father was a millionaire, who in 1921 had bought Wembley Stadium. On the return trip the starboard engine overheated and started misfiring, causing the Wellington to lose height and only just making it back to Steeple Morden. The following day Sergeant Quirk was taken to look over another Wellington which was having a new engine fitted, with the view to him flying it the following day. Later, whilst in the mess, he heard a loud explosion. It was the Wellington that he was due to fly that had crashed during its air test, killing the pilot.

Harold Coates and Vic Keeble will never forget 28 June 1942 as they, together with their ground crew, had just finished the servicing of Wellington *R1445*. With the Form 700 signed, they waited for the pilot to take it up for an air test with one of them, but, as there was to be some delay, their friend Taffy said he would go on the air test, and the rest of the ground crew, who earlier also wanted to go up for a flip, went off to tea.

After the pre-flight checks were over, Harold and Vic removed the chocks and watched the aircraft taxi from its dispersal. At approximately 5.45 pm the Wellington took off, but only did one circuit before one of the engines seized, causing the propeller to windmill and spin off. Without gaining height it crashed into a semi-detached house in Station Road, Ashwell, killing the New Zealand pilot, Pilot Officer J. E. Casey and the mechanic, Leading Aircraftsman R. L. Wilson. The occupants of the house were fortunately out visiting friends in Guilden Morden, their neighbour Mrs Revells escaping unharmed. The propeller from the Wellington was found the following day at David Hitch's farm in Steeple Morden.

The following day at 4.20 am another Wellington, *X3173*, was to crash in Ashwell, this time on the edge of the village, killing three New Zealand sergeants: J. Elliot, K. A. Hendry and Armory; two other members of the crew, Pilot Officer D. P. Wadey and Sergeant Cole, escaped with very serious injuries.

YEAR 1941		AIRCRAFT		PILOT, OR	2ND PILOT, PUPIL	DUTY
MONTH	DATE	Type	No.	1ST PILOT	OR PASSENGER	(INCLUDING RESULTS AND REMARKS)
						TOTALS BROUGHT FORWARD
ly	5	WELLINGTON	2556	F/Lt. Ellis.	Sgt. Bennett / Self	7 Landings,
	5	"	2556	Sgt. Bennett	Sgt. Lunsford / Self	4 Landings,
	7	"	2528	P/O Crooker	Self / Sgt. Ford A/G	5 Landings,
	8	"	1041	F/Lt. Ellis	Self / P/O Thom A/G	5 Landings.
	10	"	2747	F/Lt. Ellis.	Self / P/O Thom A/G	8 Landings.
	11	"	1065	F/Lt. Ellis.	Self	5 Landings.
	11	"	2710	F/Lt. Ellis.	Sgt. Bennett / Self	1 Landing.
	14	"	2747	Sgt. Smart.	Self / Sgt. Lunsday.	3 Landings.
	14	"	2747.	Sgt. Smart.	Self / Sgt. Lunsday.	2 Landings.
		"	2747.	Sgt. Smart.	Sgt. Lunsday. / Self.	3 Landings.
	15	"	4332	Sgt. Smart.	Self. / Sgt. Lunsday.	1 Landing.
		"	4332	Sgt. Smart.	Sgt. Lunsday. / Self.	3 Landings.
		"	4332	Self.	Sgt. Lunsday / Sgt. Ford A/G	3 Landings.
	16	"	2747			FIRST SOLO..
	16	"	2747	Self	Sgt. Williams A/G / Sgt. Williams.	A.P. 30 mins. I.F.
		"	2747	Sgt. Williams.	Sgt. Williams A/G / Self.	A.P. 30 mins. I.F.
	17	"	2556	Self	P/O Thompson A/G / Sgt. Bennett.	A.P. 2 C+L's. 30 mins I.F.
		"	2556	Sgt. Bennett.	P/O Thompson A/G / Self.	1 C+L.
		"	1282	Sgt. Smart. Sgt. Field.	Sgt. Bennett / Self.	1 C+L.
		"	1065	Sgt. Smart. Sgt. Bennett.	Self. / Sgt. Pettitt	2 C+L.
			2502	Sgt. Smart Sgt. Bennett.	Self. / Sgt. Pettitt	4 C+L.

GRAND TOTAL   [Cols. (1) to (10)]

..................170....Hrs.........20..........Mins.

TOTALS CARRIED FORWARD

A page from Flight Lieutenant Tim Holden's log book, showing the circuits and bumps training and his first solo flight carried out with II OTU.

(Tim Holden)

Chapter 8

Lucky Escapes

Chapter 8

Lucky Escapes

At the end of June 1942 some 2,093 hours had been flown in Wellingtons and Ansons from Bassingbourn and Steeple Morden on training flights.

On 7 July a Wellington from Mildenhall, *X3404*, force-landed at Steeple Morden after jettisoning two mines. Then, on the 10th, Caxton Gibbet, the decoy airfield, was mistaken for Steeple Morden and Sergeant Tolly, flying a 'C' Flight Wellington 1C *X9614*, overshot the decoy runway and crashed. But not all the accidents were confined to flying. On the 13th the Station Commandant at Steeple Morden, Squadron Leader Mochries, was taken to hospital in Ely with head injuries after colliding with a lorry whilst riding his motor cycle.

On the 24th a Spitfire VB from Treble One Squadron at Debden force-landed after hitting a barrage balloon cable. Later that same day Corporal Jack Redfern asked Flight Sergeant Cameron if he could go on a flying test with him. Being a keen amateur photographer he wanted to take some cloud shots, but the photography had to be done in great secrecy as private cameras were forbidden in the RAF, especially in wartime.

After getting airborne Jack moved into the rear turret to take a few shots. A few minutes later he called the pilot on the intercom and said he had got all the shots he wanted, and, if the air test was okay, they could land (as he knew the pilot had a date). What happened next is best left to Jack. 'The pilot put the old Wellington, a mark 1C No *X3221*, into a steep dive and down we went. I remember thinking, "he's pushing his luck with this old kite", when there was a terrific bang quickly followed by a bump on the tail fin above my head, and I had a fleeting glimpse of something flying away in the slipstream. I turned and opened the turret doors and looked up the fuselage. It was whipping and twisting like mad and there was a gaping hole where several geodetic panels were missing. Apparently the sudden dive had pulled off the armoured dinghy cover from starboard nacelle stowage, and due to the slipstream it had knocked a big hole in the fuselage and then hit the fin over my head; it must have been that what I saw momentarily in the slipstream. I called Jack on the intercom and told him to take us down very carefully and land gently. I turned the turret on the beam and raised the guns so the butts were down by my knees so that if it was a bumpy landing I wouldn't bash my head on them.

'As we came in over the village I saw the Litlington church tower slide past, then the aerodrome boundary quickly followed by the start of the runway. I thought, "thank goodness we are down in one piece', and almost as the thought crossed my mind I was thrown all over the turret as the aircraft cartwheeled off the runway and onto the grass, finally coming to rest on one wing tip. As I'd seen a lot of Wimpies crash and knew their tendency to burst into flames I quickly jettisoned the turret door and fell out backwards. However, the crash tender and fire truck had seen what we couldn't, that the starboard undercarriage was swinging in the breeze, and they had followed us down the runway and soon had the foam going onto the starboard engine just as the flames were

Inside the fuselage of a Mk IC Wellington. Note the geodetic construction and the Elsan toilet on the left. (*Crown copyright*)

'D' Flight Blenheim which crashed just prior to its move to Steeple Morden. (R. Saunders)

getting going. Luckily both the pilot and myself escaped without injury.'

On 31 July a message was received at 11 OTU HQ Bassingbourn that Operation 'Grand National', the attack on Düsseldorf, was on. Eighteen aircraft were to go on the raid, ten from Bassingbourn and eight from Steeple Morden. Twelve aircraft successfully bombed the target, causing widespread fires, but two aircraft returned before reaching the coast due to engine trouble and four others returned early before reaching the target, also due to engine trouble.

Some very good news was received on 2 August 1942, via the International Red Cross. That Pilot Officer King and Sergeant Holland were safe but prisoners of war, although the other members of their crew were dead. They were all from Wellington R1078 (TX-Q) ex-Steeple Morden which had taken part on the raid on Bremen on 25/26 June 1942.

On the 17th a now very familiar accident occurred at the satellite when Wellington R1407 landed with the undercarriage retracted and burnt out, all the crew escaping unhurt. But despite all these setbacks the output of crews was 25 pilots, 28 observers, 27 wireless operators, 19 air bombers and 25 air gunners.

And so into September the training continued. On the night of the 2nd/3rd, two Wellingtons took off from Steeple Morden, DV718 and Z8808. Both aircraft were on a cross-country exercise. The intention of DV718 was to fly east of the Pennine Chain and pass over the Harrogate area, but, due to bad weather it drifted off course. Instead of passing over Harrogate it flew into the Pennines. Just after midnight the 20-year-old Sergeant Pilot George Francis Ridgway probably decided to pin-point his position. The weather that night was dreadful with heavy rain and strong wind as well as a low cloud base. As he descended through the cloud the Wellington hit Blake Hill on Riggs Moor just above the village of Conistone, and burst into flames. The sole survivor of the crash was the navigator Pilot Officer D. H. Lyne, who suffered severe injuries, but was lucky to be alive after crashing in such a remote area.

The second aircraft, *Z8808*, suffered a similar fate over the Yorkshire Dales. This aircraft flew into high ground between 1,500 and 1,700 feet. The pilot, Flight Lieutenant Coney, found that he could not control the aircraft, and after a tremendous battle he managed to crash land in a remote area. Luckily the aircraft did not catch fire and although all the crew were injured they survived.

So, within thirty minutes No 11 OTU lost two aircraft within a few miles of each other. But what really happened on that fateful night is best left to Sergeant Bill Reader, the rear gunner of *Z8808*, to tell. 'We took off about midnight from Steeple Morden and flew north. The weather was appalling with severe thunderstorms, totally unfit for flying. Over the Yorkshire Dales area I spotted two aircraft just below us, and the last words from the skipper were "Keep an eye on them", as at the time, night intruders were active. I could not identify the two aircraft but probably they were two from our own station.

'Then, all of a sudden, we hit the ground, and everything went red. I must have been knocked out. When I came round I managed to crawl out of the fuselage but there was no sign of life and I thought all the crew were dead. Later I discovered this was not so. I set off in the search of help, I was nineteen at the time, the night was very dark and I was very frightened. I managed to arrive at Blayshaw Farm, it must have been sheer luck that I got there.

'The ambulance crew who collected us took us to Harrogate Hospital, they were very good and reassuring. It was at the hospital that I saw the skipper for the last time, and he was in very bad shape.' Harrogate General Hospital was where many aircrews were taken after crashing in the Dales. Several buildings had to be built to accommodate the extra patients, some of which are still in use today. The Matron at the time was Miss Phyllis Thompson, who as well as running the busy hospital, always managed to find time to write to injured airmen's relatives, as Bill Reader explains. 'The Matron at the hospital was marvellous and wrote to my mother, who incidentally at the time of the crash woke my sister and told her something had happened to me. This was later confirmed when the Rev Garnett Jones found my watch which had stopped when we hit the ground.'

How the watch came to be found was through the fact that the Rev Garnett Jones was a member of the Royal Observer Corps at the time, and was visiting a local game keeper in the area of the crash. He went to look at the wreckage and found the watch, which was sent back to Bill via the RAF. But the story does not end there. The Rev Garnett Jones was later appointed chaplain to a hospital in the Cambridge area, and while there was asked to visit a young airman who was a patient recovering from injuries sustained after his Wellington had crashed in a remote part of Yorkshire. After talking to the young airman, the Rev Garnett Jones realised, to his astonishment, that the young man he was talking to was the owner of the watch he had found on the moor!

A Wellington from 20 OTU visiting Steeple Morden.

Chapter 9

Final Operations

Chapter 9

Final Operations

On 10 September 1942 Bomber Command mounted another raid on Dusseldorf using Wellingtons from 11 OTU. Thirteen aircraft were despatched but only 10 successfully bombed the target. Eight Wellingtons from Bassingbourn and five from Steeple Morden took part, one aircraft, *DV930 (TX-O)*, crashing and burning out at Chediston, Suffolk, killing the crew of five: Pilot Sergeant T. F. Monro, navigator Sergeant J. F. Stanley, wireless operator/air gunner K. H. Vigers, air bomber Sergeant A. S. Renwick and air gunner Sergeant R. W. Freeman. Another Wellington, *DV890 (OP-G)* also failed to return.

Three days later another operation was mounted, this time the target being Bremen. Twelve Wellingtons were dispatched, seven from Bassingbourn and five from Steeple Morden. Very heavy flak was experienced over the target, and enemy fighters. Two aircraft failed to return, *DV9744 (KJ-B)* and *X3169 (KJ-X)*, both from Steeple Morden. What happened that night to *X3169 (KJ-X)* is recalled by the pilot, Pilot Officer Dickinson. 'We took off at approximately 2341 after the aircraft had undergone a major inspection, when it had both engines replaced and a new wing. An air test in the afternoon confirmed that everything was OK. But as I took off from Steeple Morden with a full bomb load and fuel I felt something was wrong, and only managed to get to 9,000 feet by the time we reached Bremen. We managed to bomb the target but got peppered by flak, knocking out an engine, some instruments and the intercom, so being unable to tell the crew to bale out I decided to crash land. Fortunately the landing lights still worked and I managed to find some heath land on which to crash. All the crew managed to escape without injury.

'As it was getting daylight we decided to find somewhere to lay low. The following day we decided to split into two groups to evade capture, the air gunners, Sergeant Jarvis and Sergeant Davey with the navigator, Warrant Officer Dow, in one group, and Flight Sergeant Akehurst, the wireless operator, and myself in the other. After a quick handshake we went our separate ways. The following day Dow, Jarvis and Davey were picked up by the Germans.

'Akehurst and myself, who were hoping to reach the Dutch border, began sleeping by day and walking at night. We decided to skirt around as many villages as possible, which proved to be rather tiresome so we decided at the next village we would walk through it. This was to prove to be our downfall, as the village turned out to be Oldenburg, a small town. Still in our flying gear we were easily identified and were soon picked up by the German civil police, but we had managed to evade capture for some ten days. We were taken to the local police station. During interrogation it was realised that the following day would be my 21st birthday, so you can imagine my surprise the next day when I was given a birthday cake made by one of the officer's wives. We were later put on a train with two Luftwaffe guards. During our journey we noticed on the carriage wall there was a map showing the German-Dutch border. Realising how close we were we

Crews being briefed at Bassingbourn before an operation. (*Crown copyright*)

Steeple Morden Airfield in 1945, note all the hard stands and T2 hangar built for the American occupation. (*Bob Kuhnert*)

decided to make our escape. Throwing our jackets over the heads of our guards and hitting them we leapt into the corridor only to be met by a party of armed German officials, thus ending our escape plans. For that little escapade I was put in solitary confinement for five months, after which I was taken to Stalag Luft 3. Later I was moved to various other camps as the Allies advanced into Germany. Eventually in 1945 I was flown back to RAF Westcott where I should have gone some three years earlier'.

On 16 September 1942 the last Wellington bomber mission from Bassingbourn and Steeple Morden was mounted with the target Essen. Nine Wellingtons took part in the raid, seven from Bassingbourn and two from Steeple Morden. The target was the Krupps Works and heavy flak was experienced over the target, one Wellington having its port engine petrol pipe severed by a burst from an enemy fighter. Three Wellingtons from 11 OTU failed to return: *DV480 (OP-N)*,

11 OTU Wellington at its dispersal. (Mr M. J. Bowyer)

the crew being Pilot Officer Grant (pilot), Pilot Officer Speedy (navigator), Sergeant Swain (wireless operator/air gunner), Pilot Officer Groom (air bomber) and Sergeant Buckley (air gunner); *DV612* (*OP-L*), Flying Officer Benefield (pilot), Warrant Officer James (navigator), Sergeant Longden (wireless operator/air gunner), Sergeant Outen (air bomber), and Sergeant Hooper (air gunner); *R1108* (*TX-K*), Pilot Officer Hoskins (pilot), Pilot Officer Goodwin (navigator), Sergeant Michelin, (wireless operator/air gunner), Sergeant Illingworth (air bomber) and Sergeant Charlesworth (air gunner).
bomber) and Sergeant Charlesworth (air gunner).

This was a tragic way to end the training and operations from Bassingbourn and Steeple Morden, as on 28 September the Air Ministry had decided to transfer 11 OTU from No 91 Group to No 92 Group, and to move it to RAF Westcott and its satellite at Oakley in Buckinghamshire. 'A' and 'C' Flights and the Gunnery Flight went to Westcott, and 'B' and 'D' to Oakley. With the announcement of the impending move the airman from 'D' Flight and a few WAAF's decided to have a farewell party in the 'Old White Horse' at Baldock, and by all accounts it was a bit of a riotous affair, with a lot of ale being consumed. This pub had one of the early juke boxes, and a very popular tune at the time was 'You are my sunshine', it was number eight on the list and was played continuously all night. When they got to Oakley they found that the Engineering Officers phone number was number eight, and whenever they asked the switch board operator for 'Number eight please', they were treated to a few bars of 'You are my sunshine'. Apparently the WAAF telephonist had been at the same farewell party. The move was to be completed by 2 October as Bassingbourn was to be handed over to the USAAF. In the meantime it was being left on a care and maintenance basis, as was Steeple Morden.

For their part, Bassingbourn and Steeple Morden had

trained hundreds of pilots, observers, wireless operators-air gunners and air gunners. Some of them were to go on and have very distinguished careers in the RAF. One in particular was Squadron Leader A. P. Cranswick, DSO, DFC, who, after his initial training with 11 OTU, went on to achieve over 100 operational sorties with various squadrons, eventually to join 35 Squadron as a Pathfinder. On the night of 4/5 July 1944 his Lancaster was hit by flak in the bomb bay and the aircraft exploded. The only member of the crew to survive was the wireless operator. When 11 OTU was disbanded in 1945 it had trained in total 1,157 crews, on some 121 courses, at Bassingbourn, Steeple Morden, Westcott and Oakley. But Steeple Morden was soon to hear a different sound, as on 20 October 1942, the 12th Photographic Reconnaissance Squadron, and on the 25th, the 15th Photographic Mapping Squadron arrived flying P-38 Lightnings of the 3rd Photo Group under the command of Colonel Elliott C. Roosevelt, the American President's son.

On the 29th, a black limousine swept through the village unnoticed by many, except Don Hitch who recalls that, sitting in the back seat, was Mrs Eleanor Roosevelt, on a visit to her son and American personnel at the airfield. Her journey to the airfield was not without problems, as there were no road

Two members of 'D' Flight in front of a long nosed Blenheim. (R. Saunders)

This type of MkIV Blenheim was used by 17 OTU.
(Mr J. F. Hamlin)

signs. On leaving the 'Hardwick Arms' at Arrington, where she had been to see a field cooking demonstration by the WVS, her driver got totally lost and stopped to ask men repairing the road. Mrs Roosevelt, winding down the window, asked one of the men directions to Steeple Morden airfield. She was told that he could not tell her as military airfields were secret. With that she asked 'Do you know who I am? I'm the wife of the President of the United States'. Not to be outdone he replied, 'Well, I'm Winston Churchill', as the limousine sped away.

On 2 November 1942 the 5th Photographic Reconnaissance Squadron arrived with nine P-38Es, but they were all to stay very briefly and by the 30th had gone, the airfield falling quiet again.

In January 1943 eighty children from Steeple Morden and Litlington were invited to a New Year's Party in the Airmen's Institute on the airfield. Later in January the advance party of another training unit was to arrive at the airfield. This was 17 OTU 'D' Flight from Upwood, their move being due to the unserviceability of their airfield. Seven officers, six sergeants and 50 other ranks arrived initially, a further 172 personnel later arriving to swell their ranks. Ten long nosed Blenheims 1s, coded *JG*, arrived by the 15th and almost immediately started training on synthetic night-flying, (which meant flying in daylight wearing darkened goggles to simulate night flying).

Just as 17 OTU were settling in a fire broke out on Royston Heath caused by an aircraft jettisoning its incendiary bombs. The Steeple Morden fire tender was the first to reach the scene and put out the fire.

Twenty-four days into 1943 and 17 OTU was to lose their first Blenheim, *L9333*, after it made a crash landing at RAF Warboys. Luckily there were no casualties. However, on 28 January at approximately 10.30 pm, they were to lose another Blenheim, *L8718*, which crashed at Abington Pigotts and burnt out killing the crew, Sergeants Mitchell and Deacon.

As a part of 17 OTU training, fighter affiliation sorties were carried out with Typhoons from 181 Squadron, and Spitfires and Mustangs from the Central Gunnery School at Sutton Bridge.

At the end of March, Steeple Morden was raised to a parent station and transferred to 12 Group, Fighter Command. At Bassingbourn the Royal Air Force Ensign was lowered, and the Stars and Stripes was raised as the station was handed over by the station commander, Squadron Leader John S. Ellard, to Colonel Stanley T. Wray, Officer Commanding, 91st (Heavy) Bombardment Group USAAF, which was to stay until 1945.

At Steeple Morden, with the Blenheim now becoming

17 OTU 'D' Flight in front of a long nosed Blenheim.
(*R. Saunders*)

obsolete as an operational aircraft, it was decided to re-equip 17 OTU with Wellington Mk IIIs and move to Silverstone. By 30 April 1943 17 OTU was gone, and the airfield fell quiet yet again.

In the village the rumours that the Yanks were coming to the airfield were rife, and after a meeting between Wing Commander Mackenzie of No 12 Group, and Major Hubbard and Major Guild of the 8th USAAF Fighter Command, it was decided to hand over the airfield to the 355th Fighter Group, which was to become one of the top fighter groups in the 8th Air Force. Their stay at Steeple Morden from July 1943 to July 1945, the influx of some 2,000 Americans into Steeple Morden and Litlington, and their part in the destruction of the German air force in the air and on the ground, together with their effect on the local population, is another story.

Postscript

Bassingbourn

Bassingbourn is now the home of a new organisation – The Army Training Regiment, which is made up from the Princess of Wales' Royal Regiment, The Royal Engineers and The Royal Signals. Most of the war time buildings remain standing, including the hangars. A small section of runway remains, which is used today by light aircraft. The control tower is now a museum, which is run by the East Anglian Aviation Society, and among its exhibits are many from when 11 OTU was stationed there, together with artifacts from the American 91st Bomb Group's occupancy of the airfield.

The control tower at Bassingbourn which today is used as a museum by the East Anglian Aviation Society. In the background are the hangars which are used for various activities by the Army. (*Author*)

One of the original main hangars at Bassingbourn, 1992. (*Author*)

Steeple Morden

Steeple Morden has totally reverted back to agricultural use with only a few of the buildings remaining. The perimeter track is now only half of its original size, together with a small section of the No 2 runway. A memorial to the American 355th Fighter Group stands near the main entrance to the airfield. The land is now farmed by four farmers, two of which, Ken and Peter Jarman, have taken a great interest in the airfield's history, and allow reunions to be held on the part of the airfield they now farm.

The building of a new memorial to 11 OTU and 17 OTU has been undertaken by the Steeple Morden Branch of the Royal British Legion and is to be dedicated in 1993 and financed by donations.

Crews Ready Rooms, Steeple Morden, 1992. (*Author*)

Operations Block, Steeple Morden. One of the few remaining buildings built for the American Occupation. (*Author*)

Part of the Main Store, now used for storing straw, Steeple Morden. (*Author*)

Westcott

Westcott was put on a care and maintenance basis when 11 OTU was disbanded at the end of the war. The airfield today is used for the research and development of explosives for the Royal Ordnance Plc. Many of the wartime hangars and buildings remain, including the control tower. The runways are no longer used as age is starting to take its toll. The only aeronautical sound heard today is the occasional landing of a helicopter. Like many old airfields, Westcott has a ghost, which has been seen near one of the hangars, wearing a flying

A blister hanger at R.A.F. Oakley now used by Agri-Mech Ltd.

jacket – no doubt the ghost of one of the many aircrews, who lost their lives whilst training with 11 OTU.

Oakley

Oakley has also reverted back to agricultural use, but still has the feel of a wartime airfield with runways, two T2 hangars and a blister hangar. The hangars are now used for the manufacture of animal feeds. The other buildings are used as offices and for the making of agricultural machinery by Agri-Mech Engineering Ltd.

Winged Memories

I too, have sailed the skies, and
watched the earth beneath.
Borne aloft by mighty wings,
o'er sunlit vale and heath;
No earthly ties, no snail-like pace
for me the eagle flight.
Carried aloft with thunderous roar,
through day and darkest night.
Up above, a bowl of blue,
below a sea of cloud;
Chased by a shadow, speeding on,
my heart is light, I sing aloud.
But alas my time is short,
and soon I must return;
Back to the brown and green earth,
for which past hour, I chose to spurn.
Now my days of light are done,
and earthbound I must be,
But my thoughts still rise and fly again,
with the men who flew with me. . .
. . .so long ago.

J. W. Redfearn – 11 OTU

In a quiet corner of Bassingbourn Cemetery is the last resting place of many British and Commonwealth airmen who trained at Bassingbourn and Steeple Morden. They came from all over the world to fight and die so that we might enjoy the peace we have today.

(*Author*)

Throughout the war Jack Redfearn was a flight mechanic but he would have loved to have been a pilot. The above poem is dedicated to all the pilots he flew with on air tests.

Glossary

AA	Anti-aircraft
AC	Aircraftsman
AG	Air gunner
ARP	Air raid precautions
Bullseye	Night Training Exercise for bomber and defence personnel
C-in-C	Commander-in-Chief
DFC	Distinguished Flying Cross
Drem	Airfield runway lighting that eventually became the standard lighting at RAF airfields
EFTS	Elementary Flying Training School
Flashing Beacon	The flashing beacon or Pundit light flashed the morse code letters for the airfield, Steeple Morden being KR.
HE	High Explosive
IFF	Identification Friend or Foe
LAC	Leading Aircraftsman
Ju	Junkers aircraft
MU	Maintenance Unit
Nickel	Leaflet dropping over enemy territory
NJG2	German night fighter unit
OTU	Operational Training Unit
PO	Pilot Officer
RG	Rear Gunner
UT	Under training
WAAF	Womens Auxiliary Air Force
W/O	Warrant Officer
W/O	Wireless Operator

11 OTU Squadron Codes

KJ	Steeple Morden Wellingtons

OP	Bassingbourn Wellingtons
TX	When formed in 1940
KH	Hurricane at Oakley

17 OTU Squadron Codes

AY	JG	WJ	Steeple Morden Blenheims

AIRCRAFT USED BY 11 OTU
AT BASSINGBOURN AND STEEPLE MORDEN

Abbreviations

FA	=	Flying Accident	E	=	Write off
FTR	=	Failed to return	T	=	Training Flight
FB	=	Flying Battle			

Wellingtons

Serial	Allocated to 11 OTU			
K2556		15.10.41.	Crashed at Bassingbourn.	
L4222		25. 6.40.	Force landed Steeple Morden.	
L4244		20. 5.42.	Taxying accident.	
L4253	18.05.40.	10. 4.41.	Shot down near Ashwell Station.	FA E
L4260	31. 5.40.	29.12.40.		
L4262	12. 6.40.	10.11.40.		
L4263	31. 5.40.	3. 4.41.		
L4266	31. 5.40.	29.12.40.		
L4270	12. 5.40.	25. 5.41.		
L4273	3.12.40.	19. 5.42.		
L4276	19. 6.40.	25. 2.41.	Crashed at Newnham, Herts.	FAT E
L4286	31. 5.40.	13. 8.40.		FAT E
L4297	6. 9.40.	6. 2.41.		
L4302	17.04.40.	18. 4.41.	Crashed at Abington Pigotts.	FAT E
L4304	16. 7.41.	27. 4.43.		
L4324	12. 6.40.	21. 9.42.		
L4239	31. 5.40.	10.12.40.		
L4331	17. 4.40.	7. 7.40.	Stalled landing.	FAT E
L4332	11. 7.41.	13. 7.42.		
L4333	18. 5.40.	11. 6.40.		
L4335	18. 5.40.	29. 5.42.		
L4338	20. 7.41.	14. 5.42.		
L4339	17. 4.40.			
L4348	8. 8.40.	9. 5.41.		
L4351	17. 4.40.	12. 3.42.	Heavy landing at Steeple Morden.	FA E
L4353	18. 5.40.	10. 2.41.		

L4355	16. 6.40.	8. 7.41.	Crashed at Litlington.	FA E
L4359	12. 3.40.	22. 2.41.		
L4362	11. 6.40.	24. 8.40.		
L4375	19. 6.40.	15. 2.41.	Crashed at Newmarket.	FA E
L4376	31.12.41.	16. 2.43.		
L4378	17. 4.40.	21. 5.40.	Crashed ½ mile from Bassingbourn.	FA
L4379	14. 6.40.	7. 5.41.		
L4380	17. 4.40.	15. 5.41.		
L4381	17. 4.40.	27. 7.42.	Collided with *DV766* & *DV813* whilst taxying.	
L4382	17. 4.40.	10. 3.42.	Swung on landing at Steeple Morden.	FA E
L4383	17. 4.40.	23. 5.42.		
L4384	17. 4.40.	12. 6.42.		
L4386	8. 8.40.	16.12.41.		
L4387	15. 4.40.	13. 8.40.	Crashed at Bassingbourn.	FA E
L4390		14. 4.40.	Forced landed at Bletchley, Bucks.	
L5706				
L7780	17. 9.40.	21. 8.41.	Crashed at Steeple Morden.	FA E
N1163		20.11.42.	Missing over the sea.	
N2747	4. 5.40.	24. 7.41.	Crashed Whaddon village.	FA E
N2772				
N2844				
N2866	18. 5.40.	10. 2.41.		
N2876	22. 3.40.	22. 3.41.	Force-landed 4 miles NE King's Lynn.	
N2887	26. 6.40.	14. 9.40.		
N2894	30. 3.40.	19. 1.41.		
N2903	22. 3.41.	29.12.42.		
N2905	26. 6.40.	21.10.40.	Overshot base and hit gun post.	
N2912	6. 4.40.	24. 4.41.	Shot down by intruder, crashed into *R1404* at dispersal.	
N2945	18. 5.40.	24. 8.40.	Crashed in the sea off Bradda Head, Isle of Man.	FA E
N2960	9. 4.40.	22. 1.41.		
N2990	2. 9.40.	24. 2.43.		
N2991	2. 9.40.	4.12.40.		FA T E
N2995	3. 9.40.	2.41.		
N3001	13. 5.40.	18. 4.41.		
N3002	4. 7.40.	28. 7.40.	Force-landed Clop Hill, Henlow.	FA T E
N3003		4. 7.40.	Port undercarriage collapsed and aircraft caught fire at Bassingbourn.	
N3005	25. 9.40.	19. 8.41.	Shot down near Barrington, Cambs.	
N3012		13. 6.40.	Ditched, near shore Orrisdale Head, Isle of Man.	
N3014	1. 4.40.	23.12.40.	Stalled on approach to base, crashed and burnt out.	
P9296	15. 5.41. – to instructional, 15. 8.42.			
R1012	23.12.40.	14. 9.41.	Crashed at Hunsdon.	FA E
R1022	11. 6.41.	16. 6.41.	Overshot base,	FA E
R1047			crashed on landing.	FA E

R1065	9. 2.41.	31. 5.41.	Failed to return from Cologne.		
R1078		25. 6.42.	Failed to return from Bremen.		
R1079	22. 2.41.	1. 5.43.			
R1081	22. 4.41.	16. 9.42.			
R1108			Failed to return from Essen.		
R1091	9. 2.41.	6. 5.41.			
R1142					
R1144	11. 6.41.	16.10.43.			
R1148		25. 7.41.	Crashed near Spalding.	FA	
R1149	30. 7.40.	15.11.41.	Crashed at Kneesworth.	FA	E
R1172					
R1174		29.12.42.	Crashed Morvil Mt., near Fishguard, crew abandoned aircraft.		
R1252					
R1254					
R1274					
R1292	23.12.40.	21. 6.41.	Engine failed on circuit and crashed at Wendy village.	FA	E
R1296	19.12.40.	3. 2.44.			
R1297			Overshot at Christchurch.		
R1299	2. 5.41.	29. 5.41.	Crashed Cranfield, Cat E.		
R1327					
R1334	29. 4.41.	22. 7.41.	Collided with Ju88, Ashwell, Herts.	FA	E
R1336		21. 6.42.	Crashed at Steeple Morden.		
R1337	21.12.40.	18. 8.43.		FA	
R1370	11. 6.41.	27.12.42.	Had been at RAE & 93 Sqn for Long Aerial Mine Development.		
R1378		19. 6.41.	Hydraulics failed and overshot.		
R1404	12. 1.41.	24. 4.41.		FA	E
R1405	2. 5.41.	3. 6.41.	Crashed approaching base.	FA	E
R1407		17. 8.42.	Wheels up landing Steeple Morden.	FA	
R1445	16. 4.42.	28. 6.42.	Engine failed on take off, crashed at Ashwell, Herts.	E	
R1600					
R1661		25. 4.42.	Crashed at Waddington and landed on sewage plant.	FA	E
R1720					
R1722					
R1723	25. 4.41.	14. 6.41.	Overshot after 'Nickel'.	FA	
R1728		9. 6.41.	Failed to return from training flight.		
R1729					
R1769					
R1780	27. 3.42.	29. 6.43.		FA	E
R3172	25. 4.41.	17. 5.41.			
R3178	16. 4.41.	19. 6.41.	Overshot.	FA	E
R3207	18. 7.40.	20. 6.42.			
R3227	17. 9.40.	7. 5.41.		FA	E
R3229	17. 9.40.	11. 5.41.			

R3231	2. 8.41.	25. 5.42.			
R3284					
S3213		26. 6.42.	Failed to return from Bremen.		
T2502	15. 4.41.	to 1943.			
T2556	11. 6.41.	15.10.41.	Crashed after overshooting.	FA	E
T2564	17. 5.41.	11.12.41.			
T2617	5. 7.42.	30.12.42.			
T2705	17. 9.40.	24.10.41.	Heavy landing at Steeple Morden.	FA	E
T2710	23.12.40.	17. 2.42.	Crashed after take off from Steeple Morden.	FA	E
T2714	27. 7.40.	24.10.41.			
T2750	11. 4.42.	24.10.42.			
T2884	30. 7.42.	26. 9.42.			
T2905		30. 4.41.	Hit balloon cable, Bristol.	FA	E
X1139					
X3169	9. 5.41.	13. 9.42.	Failed to return from Bremen.	FB	E
X3170	9. 5.41.	15.12.41.	Crashed at Whittlesey Mere.	FA	E
X3173	11. 7.41.	29. 6.42.	Crashed near Ashwell, Herts.	FA	E
X3213	18. 6.41.	25. 6.42.	Failed to return from Bremen.		
X3221					
X8793					
X8828					
X9014					
X9614		10. 7.42.	Crashed at Caxton Gibbet.		
X9615					
X9616					
X9618					
X9623					
X9641					
X9712					
X9744		14. 9.42.		FB	E
X9758	30. 9.42.	22.12.43.			
X9791	2. 8.41.	19.10.41			
X9792					
X9796	1. 8.41.	16. 3.42.	Crash-landed at Steeple Morden.		
X9803	6. 8.41.	7. 9.41.			
X9905	30. 8.41.	10. 2.42.	Crashed Harrow Green, London.	FA	E
X9906	30. 8.41.	15. 3.43.			
X9966					
W5705	30. 4.41.	31. 5.42.			
W5706	30. 4.41.	19. 6.41.	Take off swing.	FA	E
W5707	21. 5.41.	27. 8.41.	Overshot Steeple Morden.	FA	E
Z1047	22. 3.42.	29.12.43.			
Z1108	5. 7.42.	16. 9.42.			
Z1139	3. 7.42.	4. 1.44.			
Z1655	19. 6.42.	2. 8.42.			
Z8670	24. 3.42.	15. 9.42.			
Z8806	30. 7.41.	2. 5.43.		FA	E

Z8807	30. 7.41.	7. 8.41.		FTR
Z8808	30. 7.41.	3. 9.42.	Crashed Stonebeck Down, Yorks.	FA
Z8827	30. 7.41.	29. 7.43.		
Z8828	30. 7.41.	4. 1.44.		
Z8969	26. 2.42.	11. 5.43.		
Z8970				
Z9097		1. 3.42.	Missing in transit to Middle East.	
AD592		9.12.42.	Crashed near Alt Moor, Bucks.	
AD640		27. 3.42.	Missing in transit to Middle East.	
BJ585	20. 6.42.	2. 8.42.		
BJ586	19. 6.42.	2. 8.42.		
DV480		16. 9.42.	Failed to return from Essen.	
DV596			Crashed at Chediston, Suffolk.	
DV612		16. 9.42.	Failed to return from Essen.	
DV717	16. 4.42.	15.10.42.	Crashed at Brecks Farm, Maypolebeck, Notts.	FA E
DV718	16. 4.42.	3. 9.42.	Crashed near Pateley Bridge, Yorks.	FA
DV764	16. 4.42.	31.12.42.		FA E
DV766	16. 4.42.	4.43.		
DV767	16. 4.42.	2. 6.42.		FTR
DV777		10.12.42.	Crashed at Byfield, Oxon.	
DV778	16. 4.42.	25. 6.42.	Failed to return from Bremen.	FTR
DV782	25. 5.42.	19. 8.43.		
DV813				
DV814				
DV816				
DV830				
DV878		16. 9.42.	Crashed near Bassingbourn.	FA
DV889				
DV890		11. 9.42.	Failed to return from Düsseldorf.	FTR
DV916			Crashed near East Claydon, Bucks.	
DV923				
DV924	4. 6.42.	8.12.43.		
DV930		10. 9.42.	Crashed at Chediston, Suffolk.	
DV950				
DV980				
DV9744		14. 9.42.	Failed to return from Bremen.	
HF911		3. 7.42.	Force-landed at RAF Langer.	

Wellingtons from II OTU which took part on the first 1,000 bomber raid to Cologne, 30.5.42.

Serial	Code	Serial	Code
Z8808	KJ-E	DV766	OP-D
Z8828	TX-G	X9792	KJ-Q
DV717	OP-A	R1065	KJ-Z
DV767	OP-J	R1337	KJ-M
DV778	KJ-A	W5705	OP-W
R1252	OP-P	DV890	TX-E
DV764	OP-E	X9614	TX-J
R1079	TX-A	R1142	KJ-S
HF911	OP-L	R1407	KJ-N
R1445	KJ-Y	DV782	KJ-D
R1600	TX-C	R1254	OP-Y
DV889	KJ-V	X9906	OP-G
R1274	TX-D		

Wellingtons from II OTU used for the attack on Essen, 1.6.42.

Serial	Code	Serial	Code
Z8808	KJ-E	DV889	KJ-V
DV717	OP-A	R1274	TX-D
DV767	OP-J	DV766	OP-D
DV778	KJ-A	X9792	KJ-Q
R1252	OP-P	DV890	TX-E
DV764	OP-E	R1172	KJ-S
R1079	TA-A	T2502	
HF911	OP-L	DV782	KJ-D
R1445	KJ-Y	R1234	OP-Y
R1600	TX-C	X9641	OP-C

Wellingtons from II OTU used for the attack on Bremen, 25.6.42.

Serial	Code	Serial	Code
DV766	OP-D	DV717	OP-A
DV782	KJ-D	S3213	KJ-L
DV924	TX-F	DV778	KJ-A
DV813	TX-Y	R1078	TX-Q
X9641	OP-C	Z8808	KJ-E
DV764	OP-E	DV830	TX-O
R1144	TX-B	HF911	OP-L
R1600	TX-C	R1079	TX-A
R1274	TX-D	DV889	KJ-V
DV890	TX-E	R1252	OP-P
DV718	OP-H	X3169	KJ-X
DV814	TX-S	R1445	KJ-Y
Z8828	TX-G		

Wellingtons from II OTU used for the attack on Düsseldorf, 31.7.42.

Serial	Code	Serial	Code
DV878	OP-Z	DV814	OP-M
Z8827		DV596	
DV782	KJ-D	R1296	
DV924	TX-F	X3169	KJ-X
DV764	OP-E	T2617	TX-Y
Z8806		Z1139	TX-C
DV612	OP-L	DV923	TX-M
R1274	TX-D	Z1108	
DV890	OP-G	DV950	

Wellingtons from II OTU used for the second attack on Düsseldorf, 10.9.42.

Serial	Code	Serial	Code
DV890	OP-G	DV889	KJ-V
R1370	OP-A	DV923	TX-M
DV480	OP-N	DV930	TX-O
DV764	OP-E	Z1139	TX-C
DV814	OP-M	Z8970	TX-Y
X9966	OP-T	T2617	TX-Q
DV782	OP-V		

Wellingtons from II OTU used for the second attack on Bremen, 13.9.42.

Serial	Code	Serial	Code
R1370	OP-A	X9906	OP-T
DV480	OP-N	DV9744	KJ-B
DV764	OP-E	DV923	TX-M
DV816	OP-M	X3169	KJ-X
DV878	OP-Z	T2617	TX-Q
DV782	OP-V	Z8970	TX-Y

Wellingtons from II OTU used for the second attack on Essen, 16.9.42.

Serial	Code	Serial	Code
DV764	OP-E	R1091	OP-N
DV480	OP-N	N2884	KJ-Y
DV612	OP-L	R1108	TX-K
Z8827	OP-O	DV916	TX-A
X9616	OP-U		

Some of the Avro Ansons used by II OTU

Serial

N5173
N5192
N9590
N9730
R9810   17.10.41.   Undershot, hit boundary Bassingbourn.
R9847
R9704   11. 4.42.   Crashed due to violent swing whilst taking off.
DG280
DG717
DG718
DG839
DG840
DG985
DJ298